NIKOLA TESLA AND THOMAS EDISON

Two Outstanding Inventors

THE HISTORY HOUR

CONTENTS

NIKOLA TESLA

PART I
Introduction — 3

PART II
A BRILLIANT MIND
Birth of a Brilliant Mind — 9
A Significant Loss — 12
A Promising Intellect — 14
Health Complications — 16
A Reckless Youth — 18
Early Education — 20
Middle Education — 22
Higher Education — 24
Early Career — 28
Move to America — 30
Career Changes and Challenges — 33
Inventive Work — 35

PART III
A TROUBLED MIND
Unusual Experiences — 41
Mental Breakdown — 46
Strengths and Assets — 48
Controversial Viewpoints — 50
New Perspectives — 52

PART IV
A FORGOTTEN MIND
Inspiration for Invention — 57
Successes and Setbacks — 58
Impractical Ideas — 60

Visionary Abilities	61
From Breakdown to Brainstorm	63
Productivity and Products	64
A Near Miss	70
Overshadowed by Rivals	71
Death of a Forgotten Mind	75

PART V
Afterword — 77

PART VI
Additional Reading — 87

THOMAS EDISON

PART I
Introduction — 91

PART II
BORN INTO A COUNTRY OF GREAT CHANGE

Edison's disability	95
A different kind of education	97

PART III
THE TELEGRAPH AND THE START OF HIS GENIUS

Edison's curious mind	101
His path to stardom	103

PART IV
HOW EDISON CREATED THE INVENTION MACHINE

The Wizard of Menlo Park	107
The home of the light bulb	109

PART V
EDISON AND THE PHONOGRAPH

Other notable inventions — 117

PART VI
IT WASN'T ALWAYS ABOUT SUCCESS FOR EDISON

The biggest failure of all	125

PART VII
THE TRUTH ABOUT THE LIGHT BULB

The real inventors	129
Bamboo was the answer	131

PART VIII
THE RIVALRY BETWEEN TESLA AND THE "WAR OF THE CURRENTS"

Edison's gruesome experiments	137

PART IX

Father of the motion pictures	141

PART X
THE MAN BEHIND THE INVENTIONS

He lived for his work	147
Edison kept great company	149

PART XI
EDISON'S GREATEST QUOTES

The timeline of Edison's life	159

PART XII
HIS DEATH AND THE LEGACY HE LEFT BEHIND

The legacy of Edison	163
The strengths and weaknesses of Thomas Edison	166
How can we use Edison's strengths in our lives?	169

PART XIII
Remember him for the right reasons | 171

PART XIV
The best books on Thomas Edison | 175

Your Free eBook!	177

NIKOLA TESLA

THE EXTRAORDINARY LIFE OF A MODERN PROMETHEUS

I

INTRODUCTION

Let the future tell the truth, and evaluate each one according to his work and accomplishments. The present is theirs; the future, for which I have really worked, is mine.
    Nikola Tesla

Nikola Tesla is a name you may have heard. In fact, it is a name that has grown in increasing popularity over the last several years as people recognize more and more the extraordinary work he had done. When you hear the name, you likely think of a scientist who fell into historical obscurity. You may not know the details of this man, his life, the work he did, his accomplishments, or the challenges he faced.

However, if you picked up this book, you likely want to know more about Tesla, perhaps wanting to bring him out of the obscurity of your own mind.

※

This book will give a full account of Tesla's life, drawing from multiple sources, including his own autobiography, which he published in parts many years ago. It will review his life; his way of thinking - including both his moments of genius and his moments of odd or unusual behavior that many also know him for; and the work he did, which many have forgotten, but which is now recognized for its important influence on the progress of scientific development.

※

In the first part of the book, the focus will be on Tesla's life. His ethnic origins and parentage will be reviewed. Some of the escapades of his youth will be described. As a child, Tesla also faced great tragedy, and the influence on his life and psyche will be discussed. Tesla's education, academic accomplishments, and career endeavors will also be reviewed in this section. His career was met with successes and setbacks, perhaps more challenges than those faced by his contemporaries. Some of those challenges were due to political machinations and/or just plain bad luck. However, some of his challenges were due to his own troubled mind, a topic which will be further discussed in part two of the text.

※

In the second part of the book, Tesla's troubled mind is reviewed. Even according to his own autobiography, throughout Tesla's life he was plagued by unusual visual experiences. He suffered multiple "***nervous breakdowns***" during times of stress. He also engaged in behavior that might today be seen as overly regimented and compulsively routine. Today, some question his overall mental state, believing that he may have suffered from mental health conditions. Yet, Tesla credited some of his unusual ways of thinking and acting for his great success. According to his own and reports from others, he also did demonstrate particular strengths of character and mind that further helped him to succeed.

Part three of the book will discuss Tesla's history of invention, some of his most famous specific inventions, the influence he had on the development of science and technology, and the way he was overshadowed by rivals, which caused him to fall into obscurity after his death. Part three ends with a look at not only his death, but the way he has recently become more well recognized for his work and the ways that his influence does now live on, long after his death.

II
A BRILLIANT MIND

❧

Every living being is an engine geared to the wheelwork of the universe. Though seemingly affected only by its immediate surrounding, the sphere of external influence extends to infinite distance.
Nikola Tesla

❧

Every brilliant mind arrives from somewhere. The person must be born, sometimes into an extraordinary family, but often into a family just like many others. They live their life, going to school, getting an education, starting a career, and perhaps doing some very important things; often with ups and downs, setbacks and steps forward along the way. Nikola

Tesla came from perhaps relatively humble beginnings and he certainly faced barriers to overcome on his path to truly demonstrating his brilliant mind.

BIRTH OF A BRILLIANT MIND

❧

In the village of Smiljan, in the county of Lika, in the Empire of Austria, on July 10, 1856, Nikola Tesla was born. Tesla was descended from Serbian ethnicity. The region he was born in, is now part of modern-day Croatia.

❧

Tesla's father, named Milutin Tesla, was an Eastern Orthodox priest. In his own autobiography, Tesla shared that his father was an inflexible man. Milutin himself was the son of an officer in the military. Tesla's own grandfather had served in the army of Napoleon. As a youth, Milutin received a military education but chose to instead join the clergy. Tesla described his father as such:

❧

"He was a very erudite man, a veritable natural

> philosopher, poet and writer, and his sermons were said to be as eloquent....He had a prodigious memory and frequently recited at length from works in several languages. He often remarked playfully that if some of the classics were lost he could restore them. His style of writing was much admired. He penned sentences short and was terse and was full of wit and satire. The humorous remarks he made were always peculiar...."

※

Yet, there is also suggestion in Tesla's writing that his father may have been more than intelligent himself and peculiar. Tesla writes that his father often talked to himself, even carrying on animated conversations and seemingly heated arguments in different tones of voice. He notes that

> "a casual listener might have sworn that several people were in the room."

※

Tesla's mother, named Duka Tesla, was quite smart in her own right, despite having no formal education. She was described as having a strong memory and was able to memorize entire Serbian epic poems. She was also good at making craft tools and other mechanical appliances for the home. In his own writing and reports, Tesla credited his mother's genetics and influence for his own eidetic memory (photographic memory). He further states about his mother:

※

> "She was a truly great woman, of rare skills, courage and fortitude, who had braved the storms of life and past through many a trying experience.... My mother was an inventor of the first order and would, I believe, have achieved great things had she not been so remote from modern life.... She invented and constructed all kinds of tools and devices.... She worked indefatigably, from break of day till late at night."

※

Tesla was the fourth child born to his parents. Tesla had three sisters, Angelina, Milka, and Marica. He had an older brother, Dane, who was killed in a horse riding accident. This occurred when Tesla was just five years old.

A SIGNIFICANT LOSS

❦

Considering Dane's death, Tesla described his parents as *"**disconsolate**."* However, Tesla himself witnessed *"**the tragic scene**"* of his brother's death. He noted in his autobiography that

> "although 56 years have elapsed since, my visual impression of it has lost none of its force."

❦

Writing about his brother, Tesla described Dane as

> "gifted to an extraordinary degree—one of those rare phenomena of mentality which biological investigation has failed to explain."

His brother's intellectual abilities made Tesla uncertain of his own, and he wrote, "the recollection of his attainments made every effort of mine seem dull in comparison."

Further, Tesla felt that his successes left his parents in deeper grief. In sum, Dane's premature death kept Tesla from identifying, working towards, or feeling confident about his own true talents.

A PROMISING INTELLECT

❦

Yet, later in life, in his own autobiography, Tesla did recognize that, as a youth, he was fairly bright. He shared a story of a wealthy gentleman offering him and a group of other boys coins. However, the man refused to give Tesla a coin, saying he appeared too smart. He writes also of his cleverness when asked which of his two aunts was prettier—he closely examined each of them and declared one as simply less ugly than the other.

❦

As a youth, Tesla sought to feed his intellectual pursuits through literature. He enjoyed reading. It should have been easy enough to indulge his interest in his father's large library. However, his father would not permit him to read. When caught reading, Tesla's father would "***fly into a rage.***" His father also hid the candles so that there was no hope of reading in secret. Tesla, being particularly clever was able to make his own candles and would read through the night.

※

Tesla also knew from a young age that his father intended for him to pursue a clerical profession. He writes in his autobiography that the thought of this felt oppressive. He instead always wanted to be an engineer.

※

Tesla was indeed a brilliant mind. He described himself as also having eidetic memory (informally called photographic memory), like his mother. With this, he was able to memorize multiple books with perfect recall. He was also able to easily learn eight languages fluently. He was further able to perform complex integral calculus calculations in his mind alone.

HEALTH COMPLICATIONS

❦

In his autobiography, Tesla recounts having poor health as a child. He reported having three times experienced an illness so severe that doctors believed he might not live. Beyond that, he admits to also getting into "***difficulties, dangers, and scrapes***" as a result of his own "***ignorance and light-heartedness.***" This included almost drowning nearly a dozen times, nearly being boiled alive, and nearly being cremated. He reports also having been

"entombed, lost, and frozen."

On other occasions, he just barely escaped from

"mad dogs, hogs, and other wild animals."

In his later life, he was surprised that he had not only made it through all of this mishaps and ailments, but that he was also in very good health. He came to believe that his "preservation was not altogether accidental."

One may question the veracity of some of Tesla's reports on these matters.

A RECKLESS YOUTH

❧

Further, Tesla does indeed describe in his autobiography incidents that suggest his own perils were often due to impulsivity and recklessness. For example, he describes an attempt, while swimming, to scare his friends. His plan was to dive and swim under a floating structure, then come out at the other end. However, he had misestimated his plan. Three times, he came to the surface and hit his head on the structure. Each time, he was also unable to catch his breath. Being desperate, he eventually realized he would have to go to the surface and breathe whatever air he could access between the planks of the floating surface. This plan worked, and he was able to get out of what was nearly a deadly situation.

❧

Despite the terror this incident likely induced, Tesla continued to engage in reckless behavior. He recounted in his writings that just two years after that incident, he would often go swimming in the river of his city. One day, swimming alone, he found that the water was higher and faster flowing than usual. He was nearly carried over a dam wall. He was able to stop himself going over by firmly holding onto the wall with both hands, but then was nearly drowning. With no one to save him, he had only his own mind to turn to for survival. He recalled the hydraulic principle and turned to his side, which reduced the pressure of the water flowing towards him. He then moved along the dam wall to the bank. In doing so, he damaged the skin along his left side and later had a fever.

EARLY EDUCATION

❦

Tesla began attending primary school in 1861. There he studied religion, arithmetic, and German. The family moved frequently to accommodate Tesla's father's work demands. This necessitated school transfers.

❦

In his autobiography, Tesla writes about the family's move from Smiljan to Gospic. He indicates it was a "***calamity***" for him. At the time, it meant leaving the family's farm animals. In the new setting, he felt bashful and alone. Shortly after the move, he attended church one Sunday. On that day, after ringing the belfry bell, he accidentally stepped on a woman's dress train, accidentally ripping it off. As a result, his father slapped him in the face. The embarrassment of the whole situation left him so upset, he felt ostracized in the community. Tesla later redeemed his standing in the community when he repaired a fire engine hose. He reports

"I was carried on the shoulders and was the hero of the day."

MIDDLE EDUCATION

❦

After settling in the city of Gospic, Tesla attended a four-year course at the Normal School. In his autobiography, he reports that during that time, his

> "boyish efforts and exploits, as well as troubles, continued."

Reportedly, he became a champion crow catcher, due to his ability to imitate the call of the bird and method of distracting the bird while he grabbed it from behind. This lasted until one day, after catching a pair of birds, a group of birds attacked him, flying into him, and hitting him in the head, after which he released those he had caught.

❦

In the classroom, Tesla was drawn to mechanical models, especially water turbines. He took pleasure in making and operating his own mechanical models. For example, he reportedly made arrows that

> "disappeared from sight and at close range traversed a plank of pine 1 inch thick."

It was also during this time, that he conceived an idea of creating a big wheel to run with the power of Niagara Falls (an idea he was able to carry out 30 years later).

※

At age 10, Tesla started attending Real Gymnasium. He was quite fascinated by the various models of classical scientific apparatus, electrical and mechanical. He enjoyed seeing the demonstrations and experiments completed by the instructors. He simultaneously became fond of studying math and often won the professor's praise for rapid calculation. He attributes his success to being able to visualize the figures and perform the necessary operations that way. Though, Tesla admits he struggled greatly with drawing, which nearly derailed him.

※

Just after completing his courses, Tesla became quite ill. During his illness, Tesla was allowed to read and was given books by the local library to review for cataloging. It was during this time, he became familiar with the works of Mark Twain. He attributed his recovery to reading these fine works.

HIGHER EDUCATION

❦

After his recovery, Tesla continued his studies at the Higher Real Gymnasium. While attending high school, Tesla took physics. His professor demonstrated electricity and this spurred Tesla's interest in it. Initially, it seemed to him as a mysterious phenomenon. He wanted to study it and learn more. Tesla excelled there academically. Reportedly, some professors believed he may have been cheating because his performance was so strong. He was not, and he also managed to complete his studies a year earlier than was typical.

❦

While attending that school, Telsa was residing with his aunt and uncle. The household was quite rigid in its discipline. Meals were well-made, but the food was limited, as his aunt believed Tesla was too delicate to consume more. He fought a voracious appetite and suffered. He also battled malaria throughout his time residing there. However, he amused himself by frequently catching rats.

※

Upon graduation, Tesla's parents sent him to attend a shooting expedition. Days later, he learned that cholera was rampant near his home. He returned to Gospic and nearly immediately, he contracted cholera. He was bedridden for approximately nine months. Multiple times, he faced death. During Tesla's illness, in a moment of despair over his son's condition, Milutin promised Tesla he could attend the best engineering school, if he would only recover.

※

The next year, Tesla was nearly conscripted into the Austro-Hungarian Army. However, he avoided this by running away to the southeast of Lika. There, he spent time with nature, exploring the mountains. He later said this experience made him physically and mentally stronger, helping him to recover from illness.

※

After his year among nature, Tesla was able to enroll at the Austrian Polytechnic located in Graz, Austria. His father chose it, due to its strong reputation. Tesla felt highly motivated to succeed. There, he worked from 3 am to 11 pm every single day to excel. He earned high grades and passed nine exams, which was many more than required. He also engaged in extracurricular activity by starting a Serbian cultural club. The technical faculty dean wrote a letter of commendation to Milutin. It stated,

"Your son is of first rank."

Despite his honors, Tesla's father would not fully acknowledge his abilities. This left Tesla feeling quite disappointed, after all of his hard work to impress his father.

Tesla continued to devote himself to physics, mechanics, and the study of mathematics. He spent hours of time in the libraries with a "***veritable mania***" for work. There, he read the complete works of Voltaire. His professors continued to be impressed with his high level of work. However, they sometimes did not support his ideas. When challenged, he forged ahead with his own ideas.

Eventually, during his education, more letters were also written to Milutin indicating concern that Tesla was working too hard. Tesla later learned that his father was encouraged to take him out of university. Indeed, Tesla soon started to face problems. For one, he sometimes got into outright conflicts with his professors, when he disagreed with their assertions. He also got involved with gambling, eventually losing his scholarship and losing all his academic funds. Tesla was not prepared for his next set of exams and had to leave school.

In order to hide from his family that he had left school, Tesla left the area and cut off contact with anyone he knew. His friends were concerned that he had drowned in the local Mur River. In fact, Tesla had moved to Maribor for a time.

There, he worked as a draftsman and spent his free time playing cards. When Milutin learned of Tesla's whereabouts, he visited, begging him to return home. It is believed around that time, Tesla may have had a nervous breakdown. Tesla was soon forced to return home by the police, because he had been homeless.

In April 1879, Milutin died. The cause is unclear, but some believe he had a stroke. For a time after that, Tesla taught students in Gospic. However, two uncles worked together to provide funds, so that Tesla could attend school in Prague. In January 1880, he arrived to attend Charles-Ferdinand University.

Unfortunately, he was missing prerequisite subjects—Greek and Czech. He was only able to attend lectures on philosophy. He would not receive any grade for his attendance. Shortly after his arrival, Tesla again suffered a "***complete breakdown of the nerves***." In time, he again recovered with support from friends.

EARLY CAREER

❦

Being unable to attend school, Tesla left Prague for a job. He moved to Budapest, Hungary with plans to work for the Budapest Telephone Exchange. When he arrived, the company was not yet in business. He worked temporarily at the Central Telegraph Office. Once the Budapest Telephone Exchange was in operation, Tesla took on the role of chief electrician. In that role, he helped to improve the equipment and later claimed to have created a telephone amplifier or repeater. However, there is no patent on record to verify this claim.

❦

After a time, Tesla's boss, Tivador Puskas helped him get a new job. Tesla relocated to Paris to work for the Continental Edison Company. The move was somewhat overwhelming for him. He started engaging in a rigorous routine for life and work. At the time, he was on the forefront of a new industry, helping to install incandescent lighting throughout the city.

※

This position helped Tesla learn more about the practical application of electrical engineering. With his advanced knowledge for engineering and physics, he stood out and was assigned to help design and build better versions of dynamos and motors. He was also asked to troubleshoot problems at the other Edison utilities that were being built around Europe. For example, he was sent to Strassburg to work there. While there, he also worked on his own inventions.

MOVE TO AMERICA

❧

In 1884, one of the managers at the Continental Edison Company, Charles Batchelor, was transferred to the US to manage the manufacturing division—Edison Machine Works. During his transfer, he requested that Tesla should be brought to the United States too. This brought Tesla to the United States.

❧

When Tesla arrived in America, he was again overwhelmed by the new place. He initially found America to be less civilized. When Tesla immigrated he started working in Manhattan's Lower East Side at Machine Works. It was a crowded shop with hundreds of staff, including machinists and field engineers. All were working to build a large electric utility for New York City.

❧

During his time at the Machine Works, Tesla met Edison on just a few occasions. In his autobiography, Tesla describes his first meeting with Edison:

> "The meeting with Edison was a memorable event in my life. I was amazed at this wonderful man who, without early advantages and scientific training, had accomplished so much. I had studied a dozen languages, delved in literature and art, and had spent my best years in libraries reading all sorts of stuff...and felt that most of my life had been squandered. But it did not take long before I recognized that it was the best thing I could have done."

In his autobiography, Tesla writes that he won Edison's confidence by working on a difficult task. A fast passenger steamer was not working, and Tesla went to correct the problem. He found the dynamos in bad condition, but was able to repair them. When Edison learned Tesla had worked all night and corrected the problem, he gave a strong approval to Tesla.

Tesla was soon given another special project to work on. At the time, arc lighting was popular. However, it required high voltages. This was incompatible with Edison's low-voltage incandescent system. This situation was causing the company to lose contracts in some cities. Tesla was supposed to create a solution with an arc lamp-based street lighting system. However, his designs were never produced, possibly because another solution was found.

After working at the Machine Works for only six months, Tesla quit. It is unclear what caused this. Some believe he was offered a bonus for work and then was not actually given the bonus. Reportedly, the offer of a bonus may have been a practical joke, and indeed the details offered in his autobiography suggest such an actual bonus would have been unlikely. Either way, he left in early 1885.

CAREER CHANGES AND CHALLENGES

❦

Shortly after leaving the Machine Works, Tesla began working on his own patents for an arc lighting system. It may have been the designs he developed while working for Edison. He worked with the same attorney used by Edison to get the patents submitted. That attorney introduced Tesla to Robert Lane and Benjamin Vail. These two businessmen agreed to provide funds for Tesla's own manufacturing and utility company. This was the Tesla Electric Light & Manufacturing company. With this, Tesla was able to get more patents and install a lighting system in New Jersey. The press wrote about it, impressed by the advanced features in Tesla's new system.

❦

Unfortunately, Tesla's investors had little interest in some of his own ideas. Particularly, they did not want to fund his work on Alternating Current motors or new types of electrical transmission equipment. So, when Tesla got the utilities working, the investors decided to only fund the electric utility. They abandoned the manufacturing side of the business. Shortly, they formed an entirely new utility company, abandoning Tesla, and leaving him with no money.

Tesla's patents were tied to the company, as he had exchanged them for stock (stock that was now worthless). As a result of the circumstances, Tesla had to get by, by working at electrical repair jobs and even as a ditch digger. Looking back on that time period years later, Tesla said of 1886 that it was a time of hardship and that,

> "My high education in various branches of science, mechanics, and literature seemed to me like a mockery."

Yet, by late 1886, Tesla's circumstances started to improve again. He met Alfred Brown (a Western Union Superintendent) and Charles Peck (a New York Attorney). The two were experienced with setting up companies and promoting inventions. They were impressed with Tesla's new ideas and agreed to provide financial backing for his work. They would also handle his patents. This formed the Tesla Electric Company. Tesla was to earn one-third of the profits from any patents and one-third would go back into development.

INVENTIVE WORK

❦

Tesla was given a laboratory in Manhattan at 89 Liberty Street. There, he could work on developing new ideas and improving existing ideas. He was focused initially on electric motors, generators, and similar devices. Shortly (in 1887) he was able to develop an induction motor that ran on Alternating Current. This power system was growing in popularity because it allowed for long-distance and high-voltage transmission of power.

❦

Tesla's new motor worked on a polyphase current. This generated a rotating magnetic field, which turned the motor. The design also allowed for self-starting and did not need any commutator. This helped to avoid the risk of sparking. It also helped to reduce the need for servicing and maintenance. The electric motor was patented in May 1888. Peck and Brown set out to publicize the motor. They did this with independent testing, which verified its functional improvement. Then, press releases were published along with a copy of the patent.

Also, in early 1888, arrangements were made for the Westinghouse Company to manufacture Tesla's motors, on a large scale. This plan faced some challenges. The Tesla motors were based on low-frequency currents, but this did not match the standard forms of the Westinghouse apparatus. Adaptions had to be made.

Starting in 1889, Tesla continued working in New York at his laboratory. He focused on designing high-frequency machines. This was challenging work because it was such a novel field. He initially rejected a method that he later realized could have worked well. He also sought to invent a more simple device for producing electric oscillations. At the time, Tesla was inspired by the work of Kelvin. Tesla made rapid progress and produced a coil that could give sparks as large as five inches. According to Tesla,

> "Since my early announcement of the invention it has come into universal use and wrought a revolution in many departments. But still a greater future awaits it."

Eventually, the device could create discharges as large as 100 feet, to flash large currents across the globe.

In 1890 Tesla conducted a laboratory experiment on high-frequency currents to show that an electric field of sufficient intensity could be produced in a room to light up electrodeless vacuum tubes. This invention was seen as a success and viewed with amazement by the public. As his achievements were noticed, Tesla struggled with the recognition. He wanted to just focus on his work.

※

Aside from this, throughout the 1890s Tesla was very productive. He invented electric oscillators, meters, improved lights, experimented with X-Rays, and demonstrated radio communication by piloting a boat around a pool (two years before Guglielmo Marconi showed radio communication abilities).

※

In 1891, Tesla, along with Westinghouse, provided the lighting for the World's Columbian Exposition in Chicago. They also worked with General Electric to place AC generators near Niagara Falls, which was the first power station.

※

Around that time, Tesla conceived an idea to create a larger machine that could do more than any previously. Unfortunately, in 1895, his laboratory was destroyed by fire. This set his work back and he had to take time to re-build his lab before he could resume his work. He did resume and continued to make machines that could produce more and more volts of electricity. To continue his work, Tesla went to Colorado to work for a year. In the end, he created his

"***Magnifying Transmitter***," which he continued to work on and refine over time.

When he returned to New York, he got financial backing from J.P. Morgan. The goal was to build a global communications network around a tower at Wardenclyffe. Eventually, the funds ran out and Morgan was too taken aback and frustrated by Tesla's schemes to offer any additional funding. Tesla was once again limited by financial constraints.

III
A TROUBLED MIND

❦

I do not think there is any thrill that can go through the human heart like that felt by the inventor as he sees some creation of the brain unfolding to success… such emotions make a man forget food, sleep, friends, love, everything.
Nikola Tesla

❦

Reflecting on his own childhood and career development, Tesla wrote,

> "Our first endeavors are purely instinctive, promptings of imagination vivid and undisciplined. As we grow older, reason asserts itself and we become more

and more systematic and designing. But those early impulses, although not immediately productive, are of the greatest moment and may shape our very destinies. Indeed, I feel now that had I understood and cultivated instead of suppressing them, I would have added substantial value to my bequest to the world. But not until I had attained manhood did I realize that I was an inventor."

UNUSUAL EXPERIENCES

Tesla's autobiography, which is so rich with details about his life, reveals yet another reason that his successes in life may have been delayed. He indicates that as a child, he

> "suffered from a peculiar affliction due to the appearance of images, often accompanied by strong flashes of light, which marred the sight of real objects and interfered with my thought and action."

He further indicates he would picture things and scenes that he had previously seen. These visions were often spurred by hearing the associated words spoken, but then he would sometimes struggle to distinguish what he imagined from reality.

Tesla indicates these visions caused "**great discomfort and anxiety**." Reportedly, he consulted with psychologists and doctors, none of whom could adequately explain what he experienced. Tesla believes his experience may have been unique, but also something he was predisposed to as his brother had the same problem. His theory was that the images were caused by a reflex action in the brain on the retina "**under great excitation**." He does not believe they were

> "hallucinations such as are produced in diseased and anguished minds."

His argument as such is

> "for in other respects I was normal and composed."

Although the experience was distressing, it seemingly gave Tesla the idea for movies:

> "it should be able to project on a screen the image of an object one conceives and make it visible. Such an advance would revolutionize all human relations. I am convinced that this wonder can and will be accomplished."

Nonetheless, Tesla would try to combat the distressing images by concentrating his mind on something else he had seen. This was difficult because he had not seen much of the world and sometimes ran out of things to recall. His solution was often ineffective or lost effectiveness through use. What he found to be helpful was instead to go in to his vision and in this way, travel in his mind.

Although, Tesla was able to sometimes banish the visions from his mind with "***willful effort***," he was never able to control the flashes of light he sometimes saw. These usually occurred when he was in a "***dangerous or distressing situation***" or when he was "***greatly exhilarated***." At times, he would even see the air around him filled with flames. The intensity of these visions continued to increase.

Then, at age 25, he attended a shooting expedition and the fresh air invigorated him. That night, he felt a sensation that his brain had caught fire. He saw a light similar to a small sun. He applied cold compressions to his head throughout the night. It took time for the flashes of light to diminish—three weeks before they were entirely gone. He never attended another shooting expedition after that.

After that, he continued to sometimes experience these flashes of light, such as when a new idea came to mind. However, he found them to be less intense and less interesting. In his autobiography, Tesla describes closing his eyes and seeing "***flakes of green***" light, followed by "***systems of parallel and closely spaced lines***" in varying colors, followed by sparkling lights. Yet, seeing such images at night often helped him to sleep and the absence indicated a restless night.

❦

Also, in his autobiography, Tesla reports false beliefs, cognitive distortions, obsessions, aversions, and compulsions. He describes, as a child, wanting to fly and really believing that perhaps he could. He simultaneously had many "***dislikes and habits***." He had an aversion to earrings and especially pearls. In contrast, other jewelry quite drew his attention. He was repulsed by other peoples' hair. The sight of a peach would give him a fever. He would count steps when he walked and compulsively calculate the cubic contents of containers. Completed acts needed to be divisible by three, even it if took hours.

❦

Beyond these odd behaviors and beliefs, Tesla also described himself as being

> "oppressed by thoughts of pain in life and death and religious fear. I was swayed by superstitious belief and lived in constant dread of the spirit of evil, of ghosts and ogres and other unholy monsters of the dark."

❦

Telsa writes in his autobiography that after reading a book, he was able to engage in some form of self-discipline that he previously lacked. He became more able to exercise his own will. However, he then became overly confident in his abilities for self-control. As a result, he started to engage with self-destructive activities, such as gambling and smoking to which he became addicted. In time, he was able to resolve his addiction and give up his various vices.

MENTAL BREAKDOWN

❧

Writing himself about his mental breakdown that occurred while at University, Tesla says: "What I experienced during the period of that illness surpasses all belief."

He described his senses, which were always keen, as being so strong, he could hear a watch tick from rooms away. He further described being overstimulated by sights, sounds, motions, and changes in air pressure. he often found his heart racing and his body moving with "***twitches and tremors***."

❧

Later in life, he experienced other bouts of psychological symptoms during times of overwork and distress. For example, in his autobiography, he describes being so taxed with a project that he started having visions of a past life. Even as he had such visions, he continued working with a divided mind.

※

Additionally, he further came to believe that perhaps he had some psychic or mystical abilities that allowed him to predict future events and commune with his mother briefly upon her death. His scientific mind saw arguments to the contrary, but he did believe that people are little more than automatons, acted on by outside forces. He described in his autobiography having some experience of "*cosmic*" pain that he felt when himself or others were affected in some way.

STRENGTHS AND ASSETS

❦

Despite his troubled mind, Tesla was also viewed as hardworking and persistent. Writing about this, he said,

> "I am credited with being one of the hardest workers and perhaps I am, if thought is the equivalent of labor, for I have devoted to it almost all of my waking hours. But if work is interpreted to be a definite performance in a specified time according to a rigid rule, then I may be the worst of idlers. Every effort under compulsion demands a sacrifice of life-energy. I never paid such a price. On the contrary, I have thrived on my thoughts."

❦

In his autobiography, Tesla writes about the way he later dealt with physical and mental exhaustion. He reported that he never took vacations, instead when overworked and led to the accumulation of "***some toxic agent***" he would sink into a nearly lethargic state which lasts half an hour to the minute.

❧

After waking, he was always able to continue his work with a fresh mind and a way past obstacles that previously may have prevented him from progress. Sometimes, he would take a break from work for weeks or months and then return to a project to complete it.

❧

Moreover, Tesla was generally quite prone to exaggeration about his own abilities. For example, in his autobiography, he described having skin on his stomach "***like that of a crocodile***" and the ability to digest cobble-stones. He also tells a tale of being able to throw a rock at a trout that had jumped out of the water, hitting it just right so that it pressed the trout into a river rock, severing it in two. Reportedly, his uncle witnessed this, and it left him "***scared out of his wits***."

CONTROVERSIAL VIEWPOINTS

❦

In addition to having some questionable behaviors and experiences, Tesla also believed in using stimulants to aid his work productivity. However, he believed that people must

> "exercise moderation and control our appetites and inclinations in every direction."

He further believed that those who were unable to, and who perhaps succumbed to health problems or death as the result of addiction, were simply "***assisting nature***" in upholding the law of "***survival of the fittest***."

❦

Tesla believed his own abilities to control his "***appetites***" had kept him "***young in body and mind***." In his autobiography, he recounts being able to easily catch himself during an icy fall, even at age 59. He also describes visiting the eye doctor and having remarkably good vision even past age 60. Further, he reports not having any change in weight between age 35 and 60, such that his suits still fit him perfectly even after so many years.

NEW PERSPECTIVES

❧

Today, scholars recognize that while he lived and learned and worked, Tesla was likely struggling with mental health issues that were not well-recognized at that time. It is believed that Tesla struggled with obsessions and compulsive behavior that might today be diagnosed as Obsessive-Compulsive Disorder.

❧

For the most part, Tesla was seemingly able to channel his obsessive energy into his creative outlets of innovation and invention. This creativity and productive work may have largely overshadowed his mental health struggles. Indeed, the analytical mind born out of his obsessiveness may have helped him in his work. Records indicate he often worked days and nights with little sleep. He often analyzed closely technology that others just accepted as is. This allowed him to search for better and more efficient ways of designing that technology. It also led him into debates with those around him, including his professors, which was problematic in the course of his education.

⁂

His mental health also caused unusual symptoms that were troublesome for Tesla. He lived a regimented life with a daily schedule. Every day he would work from 9 am to 6 pm. Dinner was attended each night at 8:10 pm exactly. He always attended the same restaurant and had to be served by the same waiter each night. Tesla also had many physical tics and among these, he believed he had to curl his toes 100 times each night.

⁂

Moreover, Tesla is reported to have had periods of sickness, during which he would even have visions. It is believed that some of these contributed ideas for inventions or solutions to various technical problems he had identified. As such, and given the time period, many just viewed his behavior as being the result of genius - simple quirks and eccentricities or something akin to a "***mad inventor***."

⁂

Today, it is believed Tesla may have suffered from a form of high-functioning autism. Research today is still examining the genetic link between autism and genius. It is known that families with autistic children also tend to have more children with high IQ. Such links are associated with instances of savantism.

For Tesla, such a diagnosis cannot be conclusive this many years after his death. It is known that he had some behavioral symptoms. However, autism is also associated with social skill deficits, which he did not necessarily exhibit. Tesla was certainly known to be reclusive as he often shut himself away in his laboratory to work for long periods of time.

Yet, Tesla was considered to be charming and refined in his interpersonal interactions. He had few relationships, but he did have some particularly close friends. Tesla also had a wide range of interests aside from science and technology. He also enjoyed music, language, and philosophy. These characteristics are less common for someone with autism.

It will never be known for certain what Tesla's mental health picture or diagnosis would have been, if he could have been fully evaluated with today's methods for psychological assessment - whether he truly would have met diagnostic criteria for OCD and/or Autism Spectrum Disorder. However, for many, viewing Tesla in this way gives understanding for his behavior, and a beacon of hope for their own abilities to fight past mental health concerns and to still carry out acts of genius.

❦ IV ❦
A FORGOTTEN MIND

❦

In the twenty-first century, the robot will take the place which slave labor occupied in ancient civilization.
   Nikola Tesla

❦

Tesla was one of the greatest innovators and inventors in history. He dedicated himself to this work because he thought that:

> "An inventor's endeavor is essentially lifesaving. Whether he harnesses forces, improves devices, or provides new comforts and conveniences, he is adding

to the safety of our existence. He is also better qualified than the average individual to protect himself in peril, for he is observant and resourceful."

INSPIRATION FOR INVENTION

❦

Thinking back on his history of invention, Tesla writes in his autobiography about his first invention. During that first invention, he made both an apparatus and a method. It happened that, as a youth, one of his playmates had a hook and fishing tackle. Everyone left to catch frogs; however, Tesla was left behind after arguing with the boy. Tesla had not himself ever seen a hook, but he set out to make one. He did so, and then went himself to catch frogs. He was initially unable to catch frogs, but eventually did so by dangling the bait in front of a frog on a stump. He was able to catch two frogs and later taught others the method.

SUCCESSES AND SETBACKS

❦

Tesla's next attempt at invention was also intended to "*harness the energies of nature to the service of man.*" He set out to use May-Bugs/June-Bugs to power a rotor. His device was successful. However, another boy came along and ate live bugs in front of him. This sight was so disturbing to Tesla that he abandoned the project and was unable to work with insects ever again.

❦

Tesla soon turned his attention instead to disassembling and re-assembling clocks. He was quite good at taking clocks apart, but he was not as good at putting them back together. These clocks belonged to his grandfather, who was not happy with the situation and halted Tesla from working with additional clocks. It was 30 years before he attempted to work with clockwork again.

After that, Tesla started trying to make a pop-gun, with a hollow tube, piston, and plugs of hemp. To fire the gun, he had to press the piston against his stomach and push the tube back quickly with both hands. This compressed the air between the plugs and raised the temperature, which would expel one of the hemp plugs. The apparatus was successful, but it resulted in some broken window panes. His family discouraged further use of it.

After the success of the pop gun and being discouraged from doing more with it, Tesla started carving swords from pieces of furniture. This action was inspired by his admiration for the heroes of poetry. Using his swords, he would attack cornstalks, which ruined the crops. Tesla's mother would spank him as a result.

Reportedly, all of the above occurred before age 6. Then, in his second year at the Real Gymnasium, Tesla became fixated on producing a device that could be continuously set in motion by steady air pressure. He struggled for some time with putting this device together but was eventually able to create such a device. This was comprised of a cylinder that could rotate freely on two bearings.

IMPRACTICAL IDEAS

After recovering from cholera, during his year in nature, Tesla conceived of some inventions. He brainstormed an invention that could be used to move letters and packages across large bodies of water. He believed this could be done through a submarine tube, in spherical containers. He thought that a pumping plant could force water through the tube, moving the spheres along. Another idea was to construct a ring around the equator. This could float freely and be set in a spinning motion. He believed this would allow fast travel. The third idea was to draw power from the rotational energy of the terrestrial bodies.

VISIONARY ABILITIES

❧

Tesla cited his tendency to visualize items as helpful for his inventive mind. Reportedly, at age 17, when his mind turned towards invention, he was able to visualize easily without models, drawings, or experiments. He could picture things as very real in his mind, which allowed him to use a new method for materializing his ideas. Tesla considered visualization most efficient because the act of constructing an idea into reality could cause someone to rush into the work and then just get lost in the details of that construction process. He believed that overall it would diminish quality. On his method he wrote:

> "My method is different. I do not rush into actual work. When I get an idea, I start at once building it up in my imagination. I change the construction, make improvements, and operate the device in my mind…In this way I am able to rapidly develop and perfect a conception without touching anything.

When I have gone so far as to embody in the invention every possible improvement I can think of and see no fault anywhere, I put into concrete form this final product of my brain…Invariably my device works as I conceived that it should, and the experiment comes out exactly as I planned it. In 20 years, there has not been a single exception."

Tesla also credited his history of visions as increasing his abilities for observation and determination of cause and effect. Skills he could then use automatically, which helped him in his scientific and inventive endeavors.

FROM BREAKDOWN TO BRAINSTORM

❦

After Tesla's major "***nervous breakdown***" he found himself full of ideas for inventions. Spending time picturing machines and devising new ideas give him a

> "mental state of happiness about as complete as I have ever known in life."

During that time, ideas came to him in "***an uninterrupted stream***." Over that time period, he conceived many ideas for motors and system modifications—things he would later develop, that became associated with his great successes.

PRODUCTIVITY AND PRODUCTS

❧

Later, while Tesla worked for the telephone company, he continued to work on his own inventions, finding some support from those he worked with. Although, he faced setbacks at times, over time, he was able to make several inventions that were useful and influential. Among these were the following devices:

❧

Alternating Current

❧

In Tesla's time, science was on the precipice of harnessing electricity. No one could say for sure what the best way was to accomplish this task. Thus, a rivalry was born. Many most associate Edison with electricity and indeed, he promoted the DC current. This approach was more expensive over long-distances and could produce dangerous sparks. In contrast, Tesla promoted the Alternating Current, which Edison touted as being dangerous.

༺༻

To prove the dangers of the AC approach, Edison would electrocute animals in front of audiences—he had essentially created the electric chair, which was later put into use for people. In truth, Tesla was offering the AC option as a safer, less expensive choice. Although, Tesla attempted to demonstrate the safety of the AC option, Edison and his colleagues continually tried to suppress his approach. Ultimately, Tesla's approach did win out, and it now powers North America.

༺༻

Electric Lights

༺༻

Tesla himself did not invent light. However, he did develop and use fluorescent bulbs approximately 40 years before they became well-produced in industry. He also created the first neon signs at the World's Fair, when he took glass tubes and bent them into different shapes.

༺༻

The Tesla Coil

༺༻

Tesla developed the Tesla Coil in 1891 based on the idea that the Earth itself could be used as a magnet to generate electricity (now known as electromagnetism). This could be transmitted with frequencies and captured by a receiver. The Tesla Coil uses two coils, one primary and one secondary. Each coil has its own capacitor. This stores energy, similar to a battery. The coils are also connected to a spark gap, which is the area where the spark can generate. This allows the Tesla Coil to shoot electrical currents even across long distances.

Magnifying Transmitter

Tesla's Magnifying Transmitter was a precursor to other devices and was intended to be one step towards the wireless transmission of electricity. He believed completing this invention would lead to important and valuable humanitarian consequences. Considering it, he wrote:

> "The greatest good will comes from technical improvements tending to unification and harmony, and my wireless transmitter is preeminently such. By its means the human voice and likeness will be reproduced everywhere and factories driven thousands of miles from waterfalls furnishing power; aerial machines will be propelled around the earth without a stop and the sun's energy controlled to create lakes and rivers for motive purposes and transformation of arid deserts into fertile land.

> Its introduction for telegraphic, telephone and similar uses will automatically cut out the statics and all other interferences which at present impose narrow limits to the application of the wireless."

In his efforts to create what he deemed such an important device, Tesla again exhausted himself, nearly leading to another breakdown. This delayed the completion of the work. In his autobiography, he described the science of the Magnifying Transmitter as follows:

> "It is a resonant transformer with a secondary in which the parts, charged to a high potential, are of considerable area and arranged in space along ideal enveloping surfaces of very large radii of curvature so that no leak can occur even if the conductor is bare. It is suitable for any frequency, from a few to many thousands of cycles per second, and can be used in the production of currents of tremendous volume and moderate pressure, or of smaller amperage, and immense electromotive force. The maximum electric tension is merely dependent on the curvature of the surfaces on which the charged elements are situated and the area of the latter."

If this science talk makes little sense to the average reader, then it is just another sign of Tesla's brilliant mind that he not only understood it, but also wrote it.

Automatons/Robotics

Based on his ideas that outside forces work on people, Tesla conceived an idea to make automatic mechanisms that could be similarly acted on to accomplish tasks. He designed machines that could do various operations. His ideas and early works on this laid the groundwork for the field of robotics.

Remote Control

A device many people use every day, the first remote control was actually made and used by Tesla. In 1898, he demonstrated the use of a remote-controlled model boat. This device used large batteries and radio signal-controlled switches. These moved the boat's propeller, rudder, and running lights. This approach was later adopted by the military as they aimed to develop remote-controlled warfare. Although, not necessarily based on radio waves, remote controls are now widely used in every modern home for various devices.

Electric Motor

Tesla invented a motor that worked with rotating magnetic fields. This device could have been used to reduce reliance on oil and fossil fuels. However, the power and potential use of this invention was lost in the 1930 economic crisis. It was not until years later that it was put into use for many household appliances and devices. Now, it has even been put into use in vehicles that bear his name.

A NEAR MISS

❧

Perhaps almost legendary, Tesla nearly discovered X-Rays. Reportedly, Tesla and Mark Twin became good friends during the 1890s. While visiting Tesla's lab, Twain posed for a photograph. It was one of the first to be lit with incandescent light. Some short time later, Tesla invited Twain to the lab for another photo. This time, he and photographer Edward Ringwood Hewett used a Crookes tube. Upon viewing the image, Tesla found splotches on it and thought it was ruined. Just weeks later, he learned of another scientist, Wilhelm Roentgen having used Crookes tubes for X-Rays. Tesla then realized that was the error on his photo of Twain, if he had only realized it at the time, the discovery of X-Rays could have been attributed to him, rather than Roentgen.

OVERSHADOWED BY RIVALS

❦

One of the greatest tragedies of Tesla's career is that despite his brilliance and inventive mind, his work was often overshadowed by that of his rivals. These other great minds sometimes seemed to just manage to outpace him on the production of the work. As such, their names have traditionally been more readily associated with the successful outcomes. It took time for Tesla to be more well recognized for his work. Many may be more familiar with these individuals:

❦

Guglielmo Marconi

❦

Marconi was both an Italian Marquis and became an electrical engineer. He put his knowledge and training for engineering into the pioneering work of developing the technology needed for long-distance radio transmission. He is reported as the first to develop a radio telegraph system. As such, he is typically seen as the inventor of the radio. Tesla too had been working on the radio, and it is now recognized that he did actually invent the radio first. However, three things allowed Marconi to be known as the first to really make the technology work.

First, in March 1895 Tesla's lab was lost in a fire. This set back all of Tesla's projects at the time because notes and research were lost. He also lost valuable time in the race for discovery and invention, as he had to then rebuild the lab elsewhere. Second, Tesla was also admittedly on the wrong track when it came to long-distance transmission. He took the incorrect route of attempting to use electrostatic induction for radio transmission. Essentially, he believed he could vary the planet's "***electrostatic equilibrium***" to signal across long distances. Third, it is now believed that his discoveries were somewhat suppressed when the U.S. Patent Office incorrectly awarded Marconi the patent. It is believed this decision may have been influenced by Marconi's financial backers (Edison and Carnegie). Such a decision also allowed the US government to avoid paying Tesla royalties.

Thomas Edison

Edison is known for his many inventions. Most important

among these may be the lightbulb. However, he also invented the phonograph and the technology for filming moving pictures. These inventions entirely changed people's way of life and sources of entertainment. It is likely that many modern societies use technology inspired by Edison's work every single day. However, Edison was not the only person to think of such inventions—Tesla did as well.

In fact, Tesla and Edison were contemporaries. They were thinking of many of their ideas at the same time. For example, as noted, both were working nearly simultaneously on developing electric power transmission. Tesla took the approach of Alternating Currents, which Edison dismissed. He instead promoted a simpler direct-current system. Thus, began the divide between AC and DC.

In that same approximate historical time-frame, Tesla was also coming up with many other of the same ideas that would later make Edison famous. He spent several years working on a system that he hoped would transmit voices, images, and moving pictures. In this way, he was among the first, if not the first, to think of ideas that are now seen in radio, telephones, cell phones, and television. In fact, his early ideas are the basis for today's mass communication system.

Despite the important value of Tesla's ideas, some of his work never came to fruition. Further, the work that he did accomplish fell into obscurity over time, for a time. Many scholars believed that Edison's bigger legacy is not due to any particular success he saw, but instead to the sheer volume of the work he produced. He was so productive because he also pioneered a new method for innovation. Edison ran veritable invention factories.

※

In his work, Edison had dozens of workers who would each take on smaller tasks for innovation and invention. When he was inspired by an idea, he would often delegate it to someone else to figure out how to make it work. For example, when he came up with the idea to make a kinetoscope (a moving picture camera) he asked his assistant (William Dickson and a few others) to conduct experiments and create a prototype. Not only did this approach allow more work to be done more quickly, it also meant that Edison was able to maintain a more stable financial situation. This kept his workers on staff and gave him the funds he needed to continue developing even more inventions.

DEATH OF A FORGOTTEN MIND

❧

In contrast to Edison, Tesla's work was slower going. This upset his financial backers, and some withdrew their support of him. His work, although brilliant was generally less successful. Although, he continued work even towards the end of his life, he also continued to struggle with his mental health. For example, even late in life, Tesla reported to mystically communicating with New York City's pigeons. He was again unbalanced, financially destitute, and reclusively alone when he died in his rented room, on January 7, 1943.

❧

Sadly, a brilliant mind, with so much potential was never able to fully realize or see his potential. As noted, after his death his work and even his name fell somewhat into obscurity. His legacy was dimmed, while others' shone brighter.

In recent years there has been revived interest about Tesla and his work. Many people recognize the key role he played in the overall profession of innovation and invention that allows the technology available today. Many also champion him today as an underdog in the world of science and in the history books.

Today, Tesla is being recognized more than ever. For example, his name was used for the innovative electric car company Tesla Motors. The company was founded by Martin Eberhard and Marc Tarpenning. Today, Elon Musk is also involved with the company. The goal of the company is to make commercially available electric vehicles. They have been successful. Recently, a Tesla vehicle was even sent into space. This is fitting, as perhaps it will start the development for a whole new form of extremely long-distance communication.

Beyond this, Nikola Tesla is often considered a hero within the worldwide geek culture. He is depicted in online comics and film documentaries. There is even a movement to start a Tesla museum to really honor his work. In this way, years after his death, through the very inventions he dreamed up, Tesla is being honored in ways he was not really honored during his life.

✣ V ✣
AFTERWORD

※

Modern science says: 'The sun is the past, the earth is the present, the moon is the future.' From an incandescent mass we have originated, and into a frozen mass we shall turn. Merciless is the law of nature, and rapidly and irresistibly we are drawn to our doom.
 Nikola Tesla

※

Many people consider Tesla to be a historical underdog, as his accomplishments are often overshadowed by those of his rivals. However, he might also be thought of as a "***lone wolf***" in not only his personal life but also in the scientific and technological world. Uncommon for the time, Tesla never married and never had children. It seems he also had few friends or personal confidants.

※

In his work, Tesla often worked alone or with very few and only insignificant collaborators. He was able to accomplish quite a lot and left behind a scientific legacy. However, one may wonder though, what could he have done to earn greater recognition. To answer this, his life and work can be examined for certain answers he leaves behind. Some of these lessons advise on what to do and some of these lessons advise on what to do differently for success.

※

WHAT LESSONS CAN YOU LEARN FROM NIKOLA TESLA'S LIFE AND WORK?

※

Do Not Let Setbacks Set You Back

※

In his life, Tesla faced many setbacks. First, his parents, especially his father were not particularly supportive of his goals. His father tended to discourage Tesla from reading and from his intended career path. Second, Tesla faced the loss of his brother, which he had witnessed. The situation had a profound effect on Tesla and his family. He felt stifled from his own accomplishments for fear of overshadowing the memory and legacy of his brother. Then, Tesla faced many injuries and severe illnesses, each of which took time for recovery. As he went through school and entered the working world, it was not easy for him. He was sometimes not given due respect and had to somewhat start over multiple times. Even incidents such as the fire in his lab and the destruction of other equipment he had built set him back. On those incidents he wrote:

> "My project was retarded by laws of nature. The world was not prepared for it. It was too far ahead of time. But the same laws will prevail in the end and make it a triumphal success."

While every setback cost him time and energy, Tesla did not give up. He always picked up where he could, even if those parts were broken and disjointed. He put what he could back together, and built new, then forged ahead. This is a great lesson from Tesla - life is not always easy, and most people will face at least some setback during it. This could happen to the athlete that has an injury and can no longer play. It could happen to the aspiring medical student, who fails an important class. No matter what it is or how hard it is, do not let those setbacks permanently keep you from success. The only way to reach that success is to take what you have, make a new plan, and keep trying. Just as Tesla did.

Anyone can overcome the obstacles of their own mind

In Tesla's own autobiography he openly reveals the many unusual mental experiences and "***nervous breakdowns***" he had during his life. Such experiences could have also prevented his success. However, he did not let these symptoms, experiences, incidents, and situations halt him from what he wanted to achieve. He found ways to keep himself going, even if those ways involved perhaps regimented routines. Science now shows that routine can, in fact, be quite important for those suffering from mental health symptoms. Considering his own struggles and continued work towards success, Tesla himself writes:

> "Can anyone believe that so hopeless a physical wreck could ever be transformed into a man of astonishing strength and tenacity. Able to work 38 years almost without a day's interruption, and find himself still strong and fresh in body and mind? Such is my case. A powerful desire to live and to continue the work, and the assistance of a devoted friend and athlete accomplished the wonder. My health returned and with it the vigor of mind."

Indeed, if you face depression, anxiety, psychosis, or some other mental health condition, do not let that stop you from living and achieving. In many cases, with treatment and support, your health too can return, balancing out your mental state. Even if you continue to struggle, it does not mean those conditions must define you. Many people can live and work alongside any symptoms of depression or anxiety. Do not let the obstacles of your own mind keep you from success, even if they are as simple as self-doubt or perfectionism. Further, just as Tesla was so open about his own experiences, be open in seeking whatever help and supports you need, so that you too can overcome and succeed.

❦

Think beyond what you can see

❦

During Tesla's time, he was coming up with ideas that were far ahead of his time. Such ideas spurred not only his own inventions along, but also those inventions that came after him. For example, in his autobiography (written in 1919), Tesla was conveying ideas that might seem all too familiar to people today:

> "This invention was one of a number comprised in my 'World System' of wireless transmission which I undertook to commercialize on my return to New York in 1900. As to the immediate purposes of my enterprise, they were clearly outlined in a technical statement of that period from which I quote, 'The World System has resulted from a combination of several original discoveries made by the inventor in the course of long continued research and experimentation.' It makes possible not only the instantaneous and precise wireless transmission of any kind of signals, messages or characters, to all parts of the world, but also the interconnection of the existing telegraph, telephone, and other signal stations without any change in their present equipment. By its means, for instance, a telephone subscriber here may call up and talk to any other subscriber on the globe. An inexpensive receiver,

not bigger than a watch, will enable him to listen anywhere, on land or sea, to a speech delivered or music played in some other place, however distant."

Tesla conceived of this whole system that he planned to create with his Tesla Transformer, Magnifying Transmitter, Tesla Wireless System, and other devices.

Yet, it was difficult to bring all his ideas to fruition, especially as he did face setbacks. While some of Tesla's devices started to quietly revolutionize communication even during his time, including helping the government better communicate across seas; today, one might picture an Apple Watch when they read Tesla's full visionary description. In short, Tesla envisioned a world full of his revolutionary inventions that would function better than it ever had.

Essentially, Tesla was thinking beyond what he could currently see. This allowed him to develop ideas that others had not. It did sometimes lead to conflict, when he saw ideas and solutions, arguing their case against disbelievers. However, if he had not thought beyond the limits of sight and current knowledge, he would not have developed some of the great ideas that do affect the world today.

Anyone can think beyond what they currently see, and you must do so to reach a future you are not currently in. Just as you can use your imagination to develop new ideas for technology, you can also do so to move yourself beyond your current circumstances. Even if you may see limits around you due to finances, a lack of support, or some other barrier, see past those limits for a way to success.

※

Collaborate with Others for More Success

※

In his life, Tesla was a "***lone wolf***." He had few friends and no personal family of his own. He sometimes attempted to work with others, but it never seemed to go very well. When others procured him jobs, he sometimes later left, which may have been a poor political move. He left multiple jobs and was often abandoned by his financial backers. His approach was quite different from that of Edison, who did see much greater success in the proliferation of his scientific inventions.

※

It is hard to know what greater success Tesla may have seen if he had more social and professional support. Perhaps, if he, like Edison, had a veritable '***invention factory***' it would have been easier to rebuild after setbacks and easier to turn out the work more quickly. It was, after all, the slow speed of his production that often turned his financial backers away from their continued support. While it may be easy to blame Tesla for his lack of collaboratory success, one must recognize it was not all his fault. Some of it was the circumstances and his own mental health may have also played a role.

Nonetheless, his work style and success do give fair warning that collaboration is a key for success. It is hard for any one person to achieve success entirely on their own. People need the social support of friends and family. People also need teachers, coaches, and mentors. There is no great extra success that arrives with accomplishing some thing entirely on your own, instead there is just a greater risk of setback and subsequent failure. So, take pride in collaboration with others, knowing that some of the greatest minds did not succeed alone.

Even if People do not Recognize Your Work, Keep Working

During his own life, in his autobiography, Tesla recognized that his extensive work and the power of his ideas had not been fully appreciated by the scientific community. Demonstrating that knowledge, he wrote:

> "The progressive development of man is vitally dependent on invention. It is the most important product of his creative brain. Its ultimate purpose is the complete mastery of mind over the material world, the harnessing of the forces of nature to human needs. This is the difficult task of the

power of the inventor who is often misunderstood and unrewarded."

After Tesla's death there was some increased recognition of his work. For example, later that same year, some of Marconi's patents were voided as it was acknowledged that Tesla's innovations came first. The AC system was also later adopted as the global standard for power transmission. Despite those successes, they came too late for Tesla to personally enjoy the honor of those achievements. In his lifetime and today, recognition for him remains limited.

However, Tesla also recognized that the work he was doing what not just about recognition. He truly wanted to help the world. Some of his inventions were intended for humanitarian efforts. There are even reports that he turned down money and royalties, because the work and work product were his most important goals. Instead, he toiled in not only obscurity but also financial ruin.

The remarkable thing is, he did keep toiling. He kept thinking and working. He left behind inventions that did help the world. He left behind thoughts that turned into something greater in the hands of those that came after him. The recognition was not there, but the work and its effects on humanity were there.

The lesson to take from this is that even if you do not receive great recognition, awards, or even high payment for your work, if you know it is good and necessary work, keep working. This remains true whether it is a scientific endeavor, helping others, being an athlete, or whatever field you may be in where success is truly measured by not just the recognition of others, but the recognition by yourself that you have tried to do a job well done. Be like Tesla—do your best to do a job well done, even if it is not recognized now or later. Then perhaps even in some small way, you will leave the effects of your work behind.

VI
ADDITIONAL READING

Consider these texts if you would like to read even more about Nikola Tesla:

- *My Inventions: The Autobiography of Nikola Tesla* was written by Tesla himself. It was initially published in 1919 in a serial form through different editions of a magazine. It is now available in an unabridged book with all six chapters brought together into one publication.
- *Nikola Tesla: Prophet of the Modern Technological Age by* Michael W. Simmons asks whether Tesla was an inventor or an outright magician. The text examines both Tesla's veritable celebrity status as a scientist and his fall to obscurity. Simmons also examines Tesla's relationships with both friends and rivals.

- *Wizard: The Life and Times of Nikola Tesla: Biography of a Genius* by Marc Seifer provides an in-depth review of Tesla's life. This text includes not only a review of his life and work, but also photographs of Tesla from *Time* magazine.
- *Tesla: Man Out of Time* by Margeret Cheney provides another biographical review of Tesla's life and work. Cheney gives information from Tesla's full life, from his childhood to his death, and detailing his entire life's work.

THOMAS EDISON
THE ONE WHO CHANGED THE WORLD

I
INTRODUCTION

❧

Thomas Edison, the inventor of the light bulb. Except there are a lot more to the story than just the light bulb, and there's a lot more to the invention of the light bulb than just Thomas Edison. One thing is for sure that the inventor, born in Ohio, is still remembered as one of the greatest inventors of all time, and perhaps the greatest that America has ever produced.

❧

Although born in Ohio, Edison moved at an early age to Port Huron in Michigan. He was youngest of seven siblings and was born to a father who had to flee from Canada after he took part with the Rebellions in 1837. They eventually moved to Milan in Ohio where Edison was born on the 11th February 1847. He was seven when they moved to Michigan after the railroad business declined in Milan, and eventually, Edison would start working on the trains himself.

II
BORN INTO A COUNTRY OF GREAT CHANGE

"There is no substitute for hard work."

— THOMAS A. EDISON

Edison was born in 1847 into a country that was going through an incredible amount of change. The US is just coming out of a profound recession with railways taking off, and over the next few years, America would be connected coast to coast for the first time by rail. America was going through its industrial revolution including becoming one of the world's greatest producers of steel. The world was going through a rapid change as it had never been seen before, and Edison was born into a world that was looking for people like him who could progress society even further out from the dark and into the light.

❦

Massive manufacturing and agricultural increases were happening at the time. The industrial revolution had already arrived in Britain, but this was America's turn for their own change, and it would also lead to substantial population increases. In 1840, the population of America was just 23 million, but by the end of that century, the population was more than tripled to 76 million. By the time of Edison's death in 1931, that figure would change to 124 million, which would eventually lead to today's figure of 325 million.

❦

Edison was born into a country that was booming in all sorts of ways and finding its way from the independence that it achieved in 1776. When Edison was growing up, the states of America were really becoming united in more ways than the people who fought for their independence would have ever thought possible. It was changing from a country that had great potential, to the most powerful nation in the world that it is today.

❦

Things changed quickly as they already had the blueprint from Europe of how to take a country into the modern age, except America had the advantage of learning from the mistakes so was able to achieve their revolution a lot more quickly. Edison was able to take the kind of ideas that had come out of Europe and improve on them in America.

EDISON'S DISABILITY

※

Edison developed hearing problems as a young boy, which would affect him for the rest of his life. The exact reasons for the hearing loss are unknown, as Edison himself would enjoy making up tales about how it happened to him. In one story, he said it was because he got struck on the ears by a train conductor after his laboratory in a boxcar set on fire. Another story was that a train conductor had helped him get up onto a moving train by grabbing him by the ears.

※

In truth, the reasons could be one of two things, and it is most commonly attributed to scarlet fever that he had as an infant, with ear infections that also went untreated. Another possible cause was that it was merely in his hereditary as he had a family history of hearing issues. Whatever the reason was, Edison didn't let it affect him, and he was still able to hear, but with great difficulty at times. When Edison was inventing the phonograph, at one time, he decided to actually bite down onto the instrument so that the vibrations would be delivered directly to his inner ear; he always found a way.

※

Edison didn't let it get him down though, and even found reasons to be happy with his hearing loss as he said that it gave him a space in which he could think. He was offered the opportunity in later life to have an operation which could have improved his hearing, but he believed that it was going to affect his ability to concentrate in a world of much greater noise.

A DIFFERENT KIND OF EDUCATION

❦

While many of the greatest minds in history went to some of the most prestigious institutions in the world, formal education isn't something that Edison neither needed nor wanted. From an early age, he was taken out of school and taught by his mother at home.

❦

In one of the greatest examples of being wrong of all time, Edison's teacher sent him home with a message to his mother that they thought he was "***addled***" and had a confused brain. Edison's mother immediately pulled him out of school after only three months of education. It was the making of Edison, and he would read everything that he could. He was devoted to his mother for her belief in him and desperately didn't want to let her down.

❦

The lack of formal education clearly didn't hold Edison back as his ever-inquisitive mind would give him all the answers to all the questions that he needed to know. He was the type of person to question everything, and if a teacher didn't know the answer to one of his questions, he's wanted to know why they didn't know the answer. It was that drive for answers that would see him be successful for the whole of his career.

At the age of 12, he would get his first job, working on a train, selling an assortment of various items to the people on board. He was never one for a classroom environment anyway, and with the help of his mother and his own drive for success, he was already on the right path to a successful career.

From his job on the train of selling such items as vegetables and newspapers, he'd go on to use the press on the train and create his own laboratory. This connected with his fascination of the telegraph as he knew the power that it could have. He developed a tactic of telling an operator how to telegraph headlines down the line, which would leave people wanting to read the news further down the line.

This would be a taste of thing to come with a man who not only would become an incredible inventor but also a brilliant advertiser and marketer as well. From an early age, he was already showing that he could drive up interest in something; it started with headlines, then he would use that ability to generate interest in all of his inventions.

III
THE TELEGRAPH AND THE START OF HIS GENIUS

"Being busy does not always mean real work. The object of all work is production or accomplishment and to either of these ends there must be forethought, system, planning, intelligence, and honest purpose, as well as perspiration. Seeming to do is not doing."

— THOMAS A. EDISON

In the decades before Edison was born, electricity was being experimented with, but not many realized the uses it could have. Many people were fascinated with electricity at the time, and no more so that Edison who, at this age, decided to run a telegraph line from his home to of one of his friend's. It was an incredible feat for a man, but his incessant reading to further his knowledge gave him a great amount of skill.

This was still the early days of telegraphy, and it was becoming more commonly used throughout the world. The first transatlantic cable would be laid in 1866 to link America to Britain and the rest of Europe. It was a time of change where communication was becoming more successful than ever, and it was something that Edison was keen to get involved in.

A huge slice of luck happened for him out of near disaster when he saved the life of a telegraph operator's young child from the train tracks. It would put him on the right course to where he wanted to be as the operator showed his gratitude by training Edison to be an operator, which was a role that had a huge degree of status due to it being a very skilled position.

EDISON'S CURIOUS MIND

❧

A curious young man, Edison couldn't help but tinker with the instruments and make them more efficient. He wanted to increase the speed of the machines and make them better. He started to develop a modification to the apparatus, which not only improved the speed of the system but made Edison's life as an operator a lot easier too. He was still only a young teenager at this point.

❧

At the age of 15, he started to work for the Western Union who had a controlling interest in vast amounts of the telegraph system in North America. Between the ages of 16 and 20, he was employed as a traveling telegraphist by the Western Union until 1867. Edison got fired from Western Union as due to the experiments that he completed, he actually spilled some acid, and it dripped down to the desk below, which just happened to be of his boss. He had taken the night shift at the company so that he could work on such experiments, but spilling sulfuric acid onto your bosses desk is a sure way to get yourself fired.

※

Shortly after this, he moves to one of their headquarters in Boston, which introduces him to an important set of resources including to some people who all think like he does and are keen to invent like he can. This is the start of Edison realizing that a collective of minds can achieve great things, and how he can use this collective to not only advance the technologies that he wants to but also being able to attach his name to them.

※

During that time, there was a significant boom of invention, and it was almost a fashion to be an inventor. It could be said that one of Edison's inventions was the method of inventing. In Boston, he spends time in a shop near the Western Union office where a lot of inventors and entrepreneurs meet including Alexander Graham Bell who would be a great influence on him and also a later rival. At this time, he also helped to improve telecommunication with a series of small innovations.

HIS PATH TO STARDOM

❦

It was at this time that he made a couple of breakthroughs that would see him on the way to becoming the inventor that we know today. One such breakthrough was with the stock ticker. It had been invented in 1867 by Edward Calahan, but Edison was able to make significant improvements to it. The improvements came with a printing telegraphy and a mechanism which allowed all the tickers to give the same information at the same time.

❦

His improvements also meant that an operator could bring all the tickers into line by sending them an electrical signal. This saved a lot of time and gained Edison a reputation in the business world as an inventor. The stock ticket he invented continued to be used for several years before it would eventually be replaced.

Around the same time, he was working on the quadruplex. A duplex machine was already in operation whereby two messages could be sent over one wire, but Edison had worked out a way to be able to carry four messages on the same wire and thereby doubling its efficiency. For all the minor improvements that Edison had made to the telegraph, this one was very significant, and it saved Western Union a lot of money as they could send more messages without building more lines.

They loved it so much that they decided to buy it off Edison. It was the first big financial success of his career. He wasn't yet famous though, as you don't gain such fame by making improvements on stock tickers and telegraphs. It wasn't until Edison moved to Menlo Park that he would become a national celebrity.

IV
HOW EDISON CREATED THE INVENTION MACHINE

"There's a way to do it better - find it."

— THOMAS A. EDISON

❧

It was the 9,646th patent to be registered in the United States, and it was one to be able to count electoral votes accurately. It was the first ever patent to be registered by a Thomas Alva Edison, and it wouldn't be his last. 63 years later, the man would pass away, but not before registering another 1092 patents making him the most prolific inventor in history.

❧

His inventions were vast from the advancement of electrical light to the telegraph and the telephone. He invented the phonograph and was one of the fathers of the modern cinema. He moved from being in between various jobs to being a full-time inventor when he moved to New Jersey.

THE WIZARD OF MENLO PARK

❦

It was in 1876 when the man that we know today really started to change the face of invention. He established an industrial research lab, which was built in Menlo Park, which was then a part of Raritan Township. But this name has now been changed to Edison Township in his honor. He built the facility out of the funds he made from selling his quadruplex telegraph, and Edison was never shy of investing his well-earned money into other projects.

❦

He sold the telegraph to Western Union for 10,000 dollars at the time, which, in today's money, is nearly a quarter of a million dollars. It was the first successful financial venture he had and would pave the way for many more. Menlo Park was thus created and became a factory of inventors. Many people worked at the facility under the guidance of Edison, and many of his great advancements came out of there.

One of Edison's genius moves was that no-one at the facility was able to register a patent under their own name. Everything that was done at Menlo Park was done under the name of Edison, which led him to claim credit for other people's work. While he was still heavily involved in all the inventions that came out of Menlo Park, it did mean that some of his associated didn't get any joint credit when they deserved it.

Menlo Park eventually developed to the size of two city blocks, and it wasn't just a space for researchers to carry out experiments, it was also a vast warehouse, which would contain all of the chemicals and materials you'd ever need for the art of invention. That stock would include all types of animal hair and all other types of materials. It was an incredible place where minds were free to try and create incredible things, with everything right there at their fingertips.

Menlo Park was the first research and development facility of its kind, and it's the base where Edison would have many of his most fabulous ideas. The first of his significant innovations at Menlo Park was the one that made him famous, the phonograph. By 1878, the invention was known all around the world, and it gave Edison his memorable nickname of the "***Wizard of Menlo Park,***" and the facility was known worldwide as the home of invention, with many visitors coming for a demonstration of the phonograph.

THE HOME OF THE LIGHT BULB

※

Edison had his own name for Menlo Park as he dubbed it an *"**invention factory,**"* and it's clear to see why. Not only did it have the space available, but he also built an office and a library on the site, which was ever-expanding. Menlo Park was also the place where he progressed the invention of the light bulb. As 1879 turned over to 1880, on New Year's Eve Edison would give the road outside of Menlo Park, Christie Street, the honor of being the first ever street that was lit by incandescent light.

※

It only took until the summer of 1880 for the bulb to be developed enough to be produced and sold in large quantities; he converted one of the buildings of the sight into a lamp factory so that he could keep up with demand. Menlo Park served as a testing ground for all kinds of electrical systems including having a network of underground cables that were able to light up lampposts around the site.

※

It wasn't too long until Edison was lighting up homes as he established the Edison Electric Light Company and moved on from light bulbs to see what other uses he could find for electricity. He also created his own railway at Menlo Park, which ran on electricity; it ran all around the major states. In the meantime, the light bulb revolution would continue as he created a generator in Pearl Street in New York, which was able to light up an office and all the buildings.

※

While at Menlo Park, he would apply for around 400 patents and people would come to the facility to see the work in action. There was a constant stream of businessmen and investors who wanted to see what the future looked like. While never stated as one of his inventions, the creation of Menlo Park and the platform that he gave to the invention is one of his greatest achievements.

※

In 1881, he decided to leave Menlo Park and created a series of facilities across America. In 1887 though, he would build a new research laboratory that would become more of a permanent home for his mind in West Orange, New Jersey. This is where the leading research and development of his lighting companies would take place, and from this point, it is where he'd spend most of his time.

The research laboratory was massive, and Edison wouldn't have quite the same level of success or love for the place. It was too large for one man to oversee, and most of the innovations done at the facility weren't done under his own observation. It was at this stage where Edison became less of an inventor and more of a businessman.

V
EDISON AND THE PHONOGRAPH

"Just because something doesn't do what you planned it to do doesn't mean it's useless."

— THOMAS A. EDISON

The phonograph was the first of Edison's great inventions and the one that he was most proud of. It was able to record the spoken voice with the ability to play it back. Not to be confused with the record player, this was a separate device that would help pave the way for such machines. If you didn't know, it'd take many guesses to work out what Edison first said into the recording device, which was his own rendition of "***Mary had a little lamb***."

The phonograph isn't remembered very much today, but it is perhaps the most excellent work of Edison. It was invented in 1877 and was the first ever device that could reproduce recorded sound. It's quite difficult to imagine how big of a news story that would have been at the time, imagine hearing recorded sound for the first time ever!

※

It was a huge deal, and Edison toured the device around the country, and it created a buzz wherever it went. He actually took it to the White House, and there is a story that the President of the time Rutherford B. Hayes kept Edison company until 3 am and woke up his wife, this is how much he was fascinated with the device.

※

It worked by having two needles, one to record the sound and another to playback that sound. The recording needle would recognize the vibration of the sound coming through the mouthpiece, and then the vibrations of that sound would be recorded on a cylinder. In the early days, the cylinder was made out of brass before being wrapped in tinfoil.

※

The invention wouldn't be developed any further for a long time as Edison became a lot more focused on the incandescent light bulb, which he'd become known for. The existing phonographs couldn't really be sold as the tin foil was too fragile to be of any use. Finally, after 10 years, Edison turned his attention back towards the phonograph.

❦

Edison improved the device by using wax cylinders instead, which recorded a better sound and were also a lot more reliable. The devices were then available for mass sale and were sold for a price of $20, which was still very expensive in the 1890's, and they could only record music for about two minutes. Eventually, the industry moved on from Edison's invention as the use of discs rather than cylinder came a lot more popular.

❦

As a legacy though, Edison had produced the first recorded sound and made the first records company. It's a legacy that he is not very well known for today, but as you put in your earphones, hear the television or the radio just remember that it was Edison who first ever listened to a recorded sound, and he shared that gift with the rest of the world.

OTHER NOTABLE INVENTIONS

❧

Motion Picture – Often seen as the father of the motion picture, it was one of Edison's most celebrated works. The first device he created looked much like his phonograph machine. As you can imagine, it wasn't a very usable or workable machine, but it did allow him to develop the next stage. His next device worked much in the same way as those classic film reels of years gone by. A series of pictures were fed through a machine to create a movie. At the first stage, only one person at one time could see the movie, but this changed. It's another example of how Thomas Edison carved the world around us.

❧

Vote Recorder – This was to be the first of his many patents, and he was just 22 years old when he filed for it. It aimed to help legislators who were in Congress to record their votes more quickly than the usual method of the time, which was by a voice vote system. The names of the legislators were embedded into the system, and they would move a switch to either record a yes or a no vote which would send an electric current to a clerk's desk where the votes were counted.

❦

Electric Stencil Pen – If you have a tattoo on your body, then it's a good chance that one of Edison's creation inspired the device that made it. The pen was made with the intention of perforating paper which was helpful in the printing industry and could help copy documents more efficiently than ever. That idea was taken onboard by Samuel O'Reilly who created the tattoo machine, based on Edison's invention.

❦

Electric Power Meter – If you have a meter in your home that records your electricity use, you have Edison to thank for that as well. The problem apparently arose after electric cables were fed through into each home. There was no way of recording how much each house used, and therefore, no way of knowing how to bill them. He created a solution whereby zinc would travel from one transmitter to another at a set rate. The meter reader would be able to determine how much was used and how much the customer should pay.

❦

Fruit Preservation – After perfecting the method of making a light bulb into a vacuum, Edison took it to open himself to see what other uses he could have for an airtight container. One of the ways way to help with the preservation of fruit whereby it would be placed in a glass container before all of the air was sucked out of it. While it may have worked, it was more trouble than it was worth for, so people didn't really catch on. It's another look into the mind of a man who was always thinking about how to make the world easier.

༺❀༻

Car Batteries – Edison was way ahead of his time when it came to thinking about cars. They weren't even being mass-produced, and Edison was thinking about putting electricity into them. He decided to make an alkaline storage battery with the intention of running a car for at least 100 miles. The technology wouldn't match up with his mind though, and cars continued to run on gas. I'm sure he'd be proud of the battery technology in cars today but perhaps annoyed that the most well-known all-electric car company in the world was named after his fierce rival, Tesla.

༺❀༻

Concrete house – It doesn't sound too comfortable, and perhaps that's why it didn't work. The plan behind it, however, was a noble and gracious one for Thomas Edison. He wanted to create a house that could be affordable for those on low incomes. He planned the homes to be around one-third of the average price at the time. He couldn't get enough investors to buy into the project, and it never really got off the ground. It was too much of a radical step for anyone to take.

༺❀༻

Concrete furniture – Inside his concrete house, Edison wanted to put furniture made of concrete. Again, the aim was a noble one for him to make cheap and affordable furniture for those who couldn't afford it. He wanted to provide them with a long-lasting substitute that wasn't going to break. The reason it failed though was clear. Having concrete furniture would be heavy, uncomfortable, and ugly. It was a practical solution to a problem, but it was one that people were never going to be interested in.

Phonograph dolls – With Edison a lot of the time you get the impression he was a man who was so excited about what the future could bring that we wanted too desperately to bring it into the present. That can be seen with the phonograph doll, which would play back nursery rhymes to little children. The problem though was that the technology was unreliable and the sound quality was terrible. It paved the way for the thousands of talking toys that we have today.

Magnetic Ore Separator – This was built with the intention of separating low-grade ore. This would allow previously discarded mines to be reopened as Edison could extract iron ore from rock more efficiently than ever before. He invested a tremendous amount of time and effort into the project that could well have worked, but the price of iron ore fell, and Edison had to abandon a project that he thought was going to achieve great success.

VI
IT WASN'T ALWAYS ABOUT SUCCESS FOR EDISON

"The three great essentials to achieve anything worthwhile are: Hard work, Stick-to-itiveness, and Common sense."

— THOMAS A. EDISON

Edison wasn't afraid to take risks, and he also wasn't scared of failure. He knew that with inventing came the chance of things not working the way that he wanted them too, some of his ideas were ahead of their time, and some were just not able to sell. He once said

> *"I have not failed 10,000 times—I've successfully found 10,000 ways that will not work,"*

which shows his mindset when it comes to developing a new technology.

※

One of his first failures was with the electronic vote recorder, which he invented while still working for Western Union in 1868. The invention meant that officials would be able to cast their vote on the machine that tallied them automatically. He knew that the device would save many hours for the public officials that would use it and also thought it was going to be the first inventions that earned him a nice sum of money.

※

Instead, they didn't want to know. The world of politics was, and still is, a murky one and legislators didn't want a device that could affect the vote trading and manipulation that could be done under the current system. It was an early lesson for Edison, not with politics, but also invention as it was a lesson he applied for the rest of his life. He was no longer going to invent something for the sake of invention. Instead, he was going to invent things he could sell. It was a lesson that would gain him spectacular wealth, but he still wouldn't be without failure.

※

The electric pen was such an invention that he thought would have its uses as the railroad companies had a market for tools that could speed up any process. Edison wanted to make it easier for handwritten documents to be copied, so he invented the pen that had a small electric motor and a battery. The pen wouldn't deliver ink but instead would punch small holes through the surface of the paper, which could create a stencil on wax paper that then could be covered in ink and pressed on blank pieces of paper.

※

Then pen wasn't a disaster though, but it was a bit too ahead of its time as the noise and weight of the pen made it unpopular. The batteries had to be maintained by using a chemical solution, so it was a very messy affair. As other inventions were taking off, Edison decided to abandon the development of the pen and move on. Perhaps the most significant legacy that it has is the inspiration behind the tattoo machine that proceeded it.

※

In 1887, Edison had opened up a new laboratory in New Jersey and wanted to raise funds that he could put back into the facility. His idea to raise those funds was to have a change of tactics from his usual line of thought and develop products that didn't require much thought, but ones that he thought would turn into a good profit.

※

One of these inventions was the talking doll. He imported the dolls from Germany and made a smaller version of his phonograph. His idea of 'get rich quick scheme' didn't work, and the toys quickly developed a series of issues. The toys were too fragile, the voice of the doll didn't last, the voice would also sound unpleasant, and Edison quickly withdrew them from the market. Just like with the electric pen, it was perhaps the inspiration to others, which is the greatest legacy for his phonograph doll.

THE BIGGEST FAILURE OF ALL

❧

While we have only talked about small and non-damaging inventions so far, if Edison could go back and have his time again then surely he would never try and get into the iron ore industry. For ore to be smelted, the surrounding nonferrous rock had to be removed. Edison developed a system which could achieve this on an industrial scale and wanted to process 5,000 tons a day.

❧

The system though encountered a series of expensive problems. He spent countless hours trying to redesign the crushers, elevators, and other types of machines. While his other failures weren't too bad and didn't take up a great deal of time, this one was awful. It didn't damage his reputation too much, but it did ruin his pockets as it was incredibly expensive, and he didn't let go of the project until 10 years after starting it.

Edison also wanted to experiment with X-rays and see what innovations he would make with the technology and left the research to one of his associates, Clarence Dally, who completed multiple experiments using this new technology. Neither Edison nor Dally had any idea of the risks involved, which would lead Dally to have severe burns on his arms and sores all over his body, he would continue to get increasingly ill, and Edison kept him on the payroll, even when he could no longer work. Dally eventually passed away due to his radiation poisoning, and Edison never went near x-rays ever again.

It's perhaps his failures that show how Edison achieved what he did in his life. He wasn't afraid to fail, and that lack of fear led to some of the greatest inventions and advancements of all time. If he didn't try and invent the electric pen, the tattoo machine wouldn't have been invented, and if he hadn't built a phonograph into a doll, then it wouldn't have inspired the millions of toys that would follow.

If he was scared of failure too, then he wouldn't have had the confidence to achieve all the great success that he did. For all his failures, his successes overwhelm them. When you take as many shots as Edison did, then some of them are bound to miss. In the end, he will forever be remembered for what he did do rather than what he didn't.

VII
THE TRUTH ABOUT THE LIGHT BULB

"Discontent is the first necessity of progress."

— THOMAS A. EDISON

Despite what a lot of people believe, Thomas Edison did not invent the light bulb. There are a quite a few inventions that aren't very clear regarding who actually invented them, same goes for the light bulb, which has gone through numerous changes and improvements until we get the product that we all use today.

What Edison did was create the first incandescent light that could be made available to the public on a commercial scale.

Numerous people had created their own version of the light bulb before Edison came along, but no-one was able to work out how to create a light bulb that everyone could use.

※

The reason that Edison is often mistakenly called the inventor of the light bulb these days is the same reason that many people think Henry Ford invented the car. What both men did was create a way for a product that was already invented so that it could be sold to the masses. There was no point in the light bulb existing if people weren't going to be able to use it, Edison found a way.

THE REAL INVENTORS

❦

There was a man called Humphry Davy who invented the first electric light in 1802, and it wouldn't be for another 78 years that Edison's light bulb would go into production. That invention by Davy, however, was by accident and it wasn't practical. Having connected wires to an electric battery with a piece of carbon, the carbon glowed producing light. That light bulb would come to be called an Electric Arc Lamp.

❦

In 1850, the first 'bulb' was created by Joseph Swan, which was done by placing carbonized paper filaments in an airtight glass bulb. There were problems though, and the light wouldn't last for very long at all. He continually tried to develop his light bulb and made some great strides, but still wasn't able to fully crack the code.

It wouldn't be until 1878 before Edison seriously got involved with the light bulb and filed his first patent of it on the 14th October called "***Improvement In Electric Lights,***" which pushed him on the right path of achieving his dream of a commercially available electric light bulb. As with the inventors before him, Edison attempted countless amount of materials as the filaments in the light bulb,o and he and his team worked tirelessly to find it.

BAMBOO WAS THE ANSWER

❦

Eventually, the discovery was found, and it came from an unlikely source. The material he used was a stand of carbonized bamboo, which could shine for longer than any other material. This was the beginning of light bulbs being in every home, and in 1880, his Edison Electric Light Company began marketing a product that would change the world forever.

❦

While the idea of having an electric light encased in a bulb wasn't Edison's, and that's not to distract away from the importance of what he did. In many ways, you could say that Edison invented the light bulb as he invented a way for it to be usable. He took the basic premise and made considerable improvements and worked tirelessly until a solution was found.

He and his team eventually found a solution that would be one of the most groundbreaking discoveries that have been ever made. The basic bulb that works in most homes today still comes from Edison's initial design and has only ever been improved on recently with the LED light, which can last for much longer than traditional lights.

✣ VIII ✣
THE RIVALRY BETWEEN TESLA AND THE "WAR OF THE CURRENTS"

"The chief function of the body is to carry the brain around."

— THOMAS A. EDISON

❦

Thomas Edison and Nikola Tesla, both men were geniuses, but there was a rivalry there, which helped drive each other to achieve greatness. Today, when we think about competition, we think about sport and the big showdowns that can happen. In the 1880's, though two men would go head-to-head in the battle of AC/DC. For anyone who doesn't know, the famous Australian rock band's name comes from two types of current, alternating current and direct current.

❦

Edison was very much a proponent of direct current and Tesla was in the other corner supporting his favorite alternating current. It was a ***war of currents,***" but who would come out on top? It was about the idea of which type of current would be best for the new electrical era that was well on its way.

The two were very different in their methods and their ideas. Edison was a practical man who would achieve his success through trial and error with careful planning. Making step-by-step improvement until a solution was found. Tesla was more of a maverick who would have wild dreams and tried to realize them. They were to minds of genius that worked in two very different ways.

Edison's direct current was able to achieve a lower voltage from the power station to the consumer, so Edison declared that it was much safer than any other method. Tesla, on the other hand, argued that his alternating current would be able to travel over much larger distances as the flow of energy could change direction and alternate.

Tesla pleaded with Edison to give him a chance to prove it, and Edison bets him $50,000 that it could not be done. When Tesla tried to claim his bet, Edison declared that it was a joke saying

> *"When you become a full-fledged American, you will appreciate an American joke."*

The Serbian-born inventor wasn't amused and quit Edison's company; he eventually saved up enough to form his own Tesla Electric Light Company, which obviously used AC current.

❧

At this time, a man called George Westinghouse, who had previously invented the railroad air brake, decided to create a company that was going to compete with Edison. Westinghouse recognized the genius of Tesla and brought him on board and bought that patents that Edison has previously dismissed. By 1903, Tesla was harnessing the power of the Niagara Falls and transmitting that power all the way to New York, which showcased the ability of AC current to travel long distances.

EDISON'S GRUESOME EXPERIMENTS

❧

One of Edison's misadventures was to try and discredit the AC system with all his power. He had invested a lot in DC, and a change in current would change the way that he fundamentally operated, and this was something that Edison was prepared to fight for and ended up doing so in some horrible and gruesome ways. One of those ways was by developing the electric chair after New York State wanted a more humane form of execution than hanging.

❧

They commissioned the world's first electric chair, which was to be powered by three generators from Westinghouse, obviously using AC as the current. The chair gained a lot of negative press for Westinghouse, and he tried to block their use via a court order. In 1890 though, a man by the name of William Kemmier had the so-called humane honor of becoming the first ever man to be executed via the electric chair.

※

It was a gruesome death, and the electric chair was never able to provide the humane death that it was originally meant for. That was the first of over 4,000 deaths using the method. Thankfully, the electric chair is barely used today as none of the states has it as their primary method of execution. The demonstration was effective in showing how dangerous AC was, but DC would have been equally lethal anyway.

※

In another show, Edison also got the local children to collect stray animals that he could use for his experiments, hooking the animals, mainly dogs, to different types of electrical current. He would electrocute the dogs with DC, and they would still be alive, and then would kill them with AC. It was a horrible way to prove a point and shows Edison at his most driven and most ruthless.

※

Edison continued his campaign against AC by other cruel means. Topsy was a mistreated elephant who had a series of incidents where the animal had killed or injured humans. The park where she was kept decided they could no longer look after the animal and announced that it would be hung, however impractical that seems. Instead, Edison thought it would be a good idea to electrocute the elephant, again to show how dangerous AC was.

Edison decided to film it into a short film, which was to be distributed by his Edison Manufacturing Company. It was 74 seconds long and showed the execution taking place. It required a lot of clever manipulation as not only was the elephant electrocuted, but it was also fed carrots laced with cyanide and strangled once it fell to the ground. By this time, the 'war of currents' was effectively already lost for Edison, and he eventually had to concede.

AC was simply not as dangerous as he said it was, and it went on to be the more commercially used current. Edison, though, was right in many ways. DC is safer and more practical when it is used over short distances. You know the laptop cord that comes in two with the little back box in the middle? Well, that is there to convert Tesla's AC current back into Edison's much loved DC current. In many ways, both men were right. AC is the current that runs into your home, but all your electronic devices convert that current in DC.

IX
FATHER OF THE MOTION PICTURES

"Non-violence leads to the highest ethics, which is the goal of all evolution. Until we stop harming all other living beings, we are still savages."

— THOMAS A. EDISON

In 1888, Edison's laboratory developed a device that would come to be called kinetograph. Edison wanted to do to the eyes what he had done to the ear with the phonograph. It paved the way from the basic principle for the moves what we watch today whereby a series of quick images are taken and then played together to make it look like a moving picture.

He and his team designed a long flexible strip of film that would be fed through a machine and played back. They built a device called a kinetoscope, which could play these images, and people would pay a small fee to watch them. However, at the start, only one person would watch at any one time.

❧

From this, Edison created his own production company and would take short films to be sold on. Edison bought other inventions such as projectors, which helped advance the movies that his production company could show. He created America's first movie studio in 1893 called the Black Maria where he would film performers on a stage and sell the videos.

❧

Not only did Edison help advance the movie industry to what it is today but also has a curious claim of possibly being the first movie pirate of all time. He would send his associates out to Europe to collect movies that were being made and then sell them in America as if they were one of his own.

❧

While Edison didn't invent the first motion picture, what he did bring is the public imagination in America. Just like with the light bulb, he had taken on something that existed, made it a lot better and found a way of earning money from it. A lot about the film industry we know today could be traced back to Edison.

X
THE MAN BEHIND THE INVENTIONS

"The reason a lot of people do not recognize opportunity is because it usually goes around wearing overalls looking like hard work."

— THOMAS A. EDISON

༄

It was a Christmas day that Edison would marry the love of his life in 1871 when he married a 16-year-old woman by the name of Mary Stillwell. They had only known each other for two months, and 24-year-old Edison fell in love, which an employee at one of his shops.

༄

They went on to have three children together, with the first birth being when Mary was still only 18 years old. The three children were Marion Estelle, Thomas Alva Jr., and William Leslie who would all go on to live long lives, with the youngest William being an inventor himself, graduating from Yale in 1900.

❧

Unfortunately, however, his wife Mary would not go on to live a long life and would die tragically at just 29 of unknown causes. It is thought that the cause of death could have either been from a brain tumor or a morphine overdose. At that time, morphine was prescribed by doctors for some various causes, and it could have been too much for her body to take.

❧

Edison was a driven and obsessive man who would more likely be seen in the laboratory than with his family. His families' loss was the worlds gain considering the impact that he had on the world. Edison would marry again, however, when he was 39 years old, again to a much younger woman. This time it was to the 20-year-old Mina Miller who would go on to eventually outlive Edison as she passed away in 1947.

❧

When they first started dating, Edison actually taught Mina Morse code. Despite Edison's long hours of work and his dedication to his profession, their relationship was a very loving one, and when Edison came to propose to Mina, he did so by tapping out

"will you marry me?"

on the palm of her hand. Mina had thankfully remembered what Edison had taught her and understood the message, responding back with a "***yes.***" They also had nicknames for each other with Mina calling him "***dearie***" and Edison calling her "***billie.***"

❦

One story does show the balance that Edison had between love and invention when he combined the two to do something for his wife. Mina was a lover of nature and especially bird watching. In the winter, however, the water in the bird feeders outside their bedroom would freeze over, and therefore, the birds would not come. Edison decided he would solve this issue by feeding an electrical line into the birdhouse so that the water could be heated. There was a switch in the bedroom that could be flicked so that Mina could continue one of her favorite hobbies.

❦

Edison had three more children with her, and that's where it would end for Edison, with his 6 children in total, with Madeleine, Charles, and Theodore Miller adding to the three that he had with Mary. All three of his children with Mina had notable lives. Madeleine would go to marry one of the pioneers of airplane manufacturing in John Sloane, Charles became the Governor of New Jersey from 1941 until 1944 and would take over his father's company after his death, and Theodore would graduate from MIT in physics and would go on to register over 80 patents himself.

HE LIVED FOR HIS WORK

❦

Edison was a free spirit in many ways and a free spirit who seemingly only wanted to do what he wanted to do. This would involve working for over 90 hours a week at times, and he'd expect the people who worked for his company to be as equally devoted to their work. He enjoyed his role as an inventor and also enjoyed having a team around him who were equally of the same mindset who would help him achieve his goals.

❦

He wasn't one for meaningless social engagements, even when his wife Mina would arrange formal dinners that the couple would host at their Glenmont mansion in New York. There were often times where he would feign indigestion to get out of such engagements; sometimes he pretended this indigestion even before he had eaten any food. He would make his way through the kitchen out of sight, grab some food to feed his appetite and then retire to his living quarters by sneaking off up the servant's stairs so that he could carry on inventing.

❧

He did sometimes find the time, however, to mix his work with his family life. He would often use his children to get reference materials from their library. The children would go off, find the information he needed and create a note on paper so that he could read the information that he needed. He had desks at his home with Mina that were side-to-side whereby he could study, and she could deal with all the social elements of Edison's life.

❧

At the mansion, approximately 4-6 servants were working there at any one time. If they were hosting a big event, then there was room enough for that number to quadruple. The working conditions at the Edison mansion weren't severe at all as the pay was good and there were also room and board available. Edison affectionately referred to his staff as the "league of nations" on account of the number of different nationalities between them.

❧

At one time, a number of the staff were from Scandinavia and on one Christmas Mina ordered in a Swedish candle box Christmas tree to honor their hard work at the mansion. The Edison family also had no special requirements on the staff sleeping on different floors, and their son Charles actually occupied what was meant to be a guest bedroom.

EDISON KEPT GREAT COMPANY

❊

The mansion was a popular residence and hosted a number of well-known guests including most frequently Henry Ford and his wife, Clara. Other notable guests were the Kings of both Siam and Sweden as well as another great inventor in Orville Wright. Also at the property stayed presidents Hoover and Wilson, which shows what kind of regard Edison was held in. While not always being the most sociable of figures, Edison did love surrounding himself with great minds of the time.

❊

Edison tried to keep his religious beliefs quiet and would rarely discuss them. He once said

> "Nature is what we know. We do not know the gods of religions. And nature is not kind, or merciful, or loving. If God made me, the fabled God of the three qualities of

> *which I spoke: mercy, kindness, love; he also made the fish I catch and eat. And where do his mercy, kindness, and love for that fish come in? No; nature made us, nature did it all, not the gods of the religions."*

which makes it sound as though Edison was an atheist, but he later distanced himself from that idea.

❧

Later he would say that

> *"You have misunderstood the whole article because you jumped to the conclusion that it denies the existence of God. There is no such denial, what you call God, I call nature,"*

and while he didn't like to talk about it, it does seem as though Edison believed in a supernatural being, but not God as such.

❧

Despite his showing with the elephant and his advancement of the electric chair, Edison wasn't a man who believed in violence in general. He was once asked to serve as a Naval Consultant during World War 1 but would only do so if he was able to work on defensive weapons later stating that he was proud to have never invented weapons to kill.

XI
EDISON'S GREATEST QUOTES

"The best thinking has been done in solitude. The worst has been done in turmoil."

— THOMAS A. EDISON

☙❧

Edison was a man who was able to deliver some of the greatest quotes of all time that can still be applied today. Some of them are funny, while others show his dedication to hard work. He would often use the sound bite to promote his inventions and himself.

☙❧

"Our greatest weakness lies in giving up. The most certain way to succeed is always to try just one more time."

This quote is an insight into the mindset of the man, his drive to find a filament for the light bulb was relentless and tried hundreds of different ideas.

"I start where the last man left off."

Again, while Edison is famously credited with the invention of the light bulb, he simply picked up from where the last person left off and made something better. A lot of Edison's greatest achievements were advancements on other work.

"Just because something doesn't do what you planned it to do doesn't mean it's useless."

The mind of an inventor is to think about things from new angles that no one else could have thought of. Edison was able to learn from his mistakes and used those lessons to make his inventions even better.

"If we did all the things we are capable of, we would literally astound ourselves."

Edison was a man who had complete faith in himself if he worked hard enough. His belief most likely came from his mother who believed in her son, even when his school didn't.

> *"When you have exhausted all possibilities, remember this: you haven't."*

Who would have thought to use bamboo? Edison showed with his discovery that he was willing to go to lengths that no one else would go. When others would lose hope, Edison wouldn't.

☙❧

> *"Opportunity is missed by most people because it is dressed in overalls and looks like work."*

A lot of Edison's quotes are around the premise of hard work. He wasn't a maverick genius, but a genius of the method - trial and error. It wasn't glamorous at times, but it worked.

☙❧

> *"The three great essentials to achieve anything worthwhile are hard work, stick-to-itiveness, and common sense."*

They aren't groundbreaking essentials, but Edison had each of them in abundance. He would never stop until he got the answer he wanted, sometimes to his detriment.

☙❧

> *"Genius is one percent inspiration and ninety-nine percent perspiration."*

Perhaps his most famous quote. All the memorable geniuses we know today worked extremely hard. While their minds may have worked in ways that most people's can't, they couldn't have achieved what they did without hard work.

※

"Results! Why, man, I have gotten a lot of results. I know several thousand things that won't work."

According to one of Edison's associates, around 1,600 attempts were made for a light bulb filament before the correct one was found. You could count that as 1,599 mistakes, but they all didn't matter when that one success came.

※

"Many of life's failures are people who did not realize how close they were to success when they gave up."

To achieve anything, you need perseverance, and no one knew that more than Thomas Edison. We would keep going until he found the answer.

※

"Everything comes to him who hustles while he waits."

Perhaps one of his more philosophical quotes, Edison's mind never really switched off the task, and he was always thinking about his work.

※

"Being busy does not always mean real work. The object of all

> *work is production or accomplishment, and to either of these ends, there must be forethought, system, planning, intelligence, and honest purpose, as well as perspiration. Seeming to do is not doing."*

Edison's invention factory at Menlo Park was like a production line of ideas; it enabled everyone a great space to think in which to be productive at all times.

☙❧

> *"Your worth consists in what you are and not in what you have."*

This is a wise quote from a man who did have everything. He didn't let his money change him though and continued to be an incredibly hard worker.

☙❧

> *"I never did anything by accident, nor did any of my inventions come by accident; they came by work."*

As with any inventor, there are times where Edison had his slices of luck. You only get to that position through hard work, and he deserved all of the luck he got.

☙❧

> *"I have not failed. I've just found 10,000 ways that won't work."*

It's hard to describe something as a failure if it is just a means to success. Edison used the trial and error method on numerous occasions to achieve what he wanted to.

❦

"To have a great idea, have a lot of them."

Imagine all the terrible ideas Edison had. His mind would have been working overtime at all time, and I'm sure he had a lot of thought for ideas that were terrible, then ever so often, a great one would come into his head.

❦

"One might think that the money value of an invention constitutes its reward to the man who loves his work. But...I continue to find my greatest pleasure, and so my reward, in the work that precedes what the world calls success."

Edison never stopped, he made a fortune at an early age, yet never lost that desire of will for invention, and he never let his money change his attitude.

❦

"There's a way to do it better. Find it."

This quote makes you wonder what he would think about the world we know today. A world of LED light bulbs, smartphones and 3D cinema. He found a better way to do almost everything, and the world took on that baton and improved it even more.

※

"What you are will show in what you do."

What did Edison did was leave a legacy of two woman and six children who loved him dearly. He also left behind a world that was much improved from the one he found.

※

"I never did a day's work in my life. It was all fun."

A great quote from a man who worked incredibly hard, but did so with a purpose and an aim. His drive made him become one of the greatest inventors of all-time.

※

These quotes show a man who had all his priorities in place. He knew the value of hard work, but also knew that there was a lot more to life than electricity. He continues to be an inspiration to many, he earned all of his opportunities and then made the most of them.

THE TIMELINE OF EDISON'S LIFE

- 1847 – Edison was born on February 11 in Ohio.
- 1859 – At the age of just 12, he starts selling newspapers and other items on a train that went through Port Huron, Michigan, and Detriot. He would continue to do this for four years.
- 1864 – Starts working as a traveling telegrapher before ending up in Boston.
- 1868 – Registers his first patent, which was an automatic vote counter.
- 1869 – Works on a stock ticker, which would be his first source of significant income.
- 1871 – Marries his first wife, Mary Stillwell, on Christmas Day. They would have children in 1873, 1876, and 1878 before she later died in 1884.
- 1874 – Invents the quadruplex telegraph, which he would sell to Western Union later that year for $10,000.

- 1876 – Opens up Menlo Park in New Jersey that would be the base for many of his great inventions.
- 1877 – Invented the first basic phonograph, the invention that first made him famous.
- 1879 – Creates the world's first useable incandescent light and would continue perfecting the idea, later famously generating power from Pearl Street Station in New York in 1882, the first commercial central power plant in America.
- 1885 – Nikola Tesla quits Edison's company, effectively starting the ball rolling what would become the "war of the currents" two years later.
- 1886 – Marries his second wife, Mina Miller, following the death of Mary two years earlier. They would have children in 1888, 1890, and 1898. They were married until Edison passed away.
- 1887 – Opens up his new research laboratory in West Orange, New Jersey.
- 1888 – Develops the first motion picture.
- 1892 – Creates the company Edison General Electric.

XII
HIS DEATH AND THE LEGACY HE LEFT BEHIND

"Show me a thoroughly satisfied man and I will show you a failure."

— THOMAS A. EDISON

In his final years, Edison's health began to suffer as he struggled with diabetes. He would end up dying due to complications with the condition on October 18, 1931. He died at his home in New Jersey and would later be buried just behind it as well. He was 84 at the time and was still working for as long as he possibly could.

Quite curiously, there is a test tube at The Henry Ford

Museum near Detriot, which apparently contains the last breath of Thomas Edison as apparently Ford convinced Edison's son Charles to seal it in a tube as a monument to his life. A plaster death mask was also made of his face as well as casts of his hands.

❦

In a touching moment after his death, many people and companies around the world dimmed their lights for a minute in honor of the great man who made it possible for light bulbs to be shining all around the world.

THE LEGACY OF EDISON

※

Edison's legacy is one of a brilliant man who changed the world and made much advancement to bring forward the world that we see today. He is credited with things that he didn't achieve, but what he did accomplish was incredible. He will forever be most associated with the light bulb, and for a good reason. Most advancements are pivotal to the world that follows them, and Edison's devotion to perfecting the incandescent light bulb enabled society to move on and create an even more incredible world.

※

While many of the greatest minds of all time were reclusive or at least introverted, Edison was a man who understood the value of what everyone else around him could help him achieve. With that team, he was able to do incredible things. Mass production has only recently been delivered to the industrial world, and Edison took these same principles and applied them to inventing, allowing great minds to come together to achieve great things.

※

This was a rags-to-riches story and one of the greatest to be told. He was the personification of the American dream; his father had to flee out of Canada to Ohio, he developed hearing problems, his teacher said that he was addled, and he started working before he was even a teenager. To overcome what he did and to achieve what he did was an incredible achievement.

※

There are times when he wouldn't be a nice man, he demanded a lot from his employees and would happily crush his rivals like he tried to do with Westinghouse. He had an enormous ego, but one that was justified in many respects. He had a brilliant mind and a large family around him.

※

The way that the man is often portrayed in the modern day is one of the most complicated man who doesn't deserve the credit that he gets. His popularity has decreased, and at times, it seems like it has almost become a fashion to discredit him and point to all the negatives aspects of both his character and his inventions. The same people seem to love talking up Tesla and what he achieved.

※

It is true that Edison is wrongly attributed to some inventions, and it is true that he took credit at times for work that wasn't his, but it'd be wrong to stop there. What needs to be remembered is what the man actually did achieve. The advancement of the telegraph, the invention of the phonograph, and taking light bulbs to the masses to name just a small few.

※

Despite the negative press at the time, Edison's legacy is secured for a long time to come. If it weren't for him, we just wouldn't be living in the same world. Even if you consider what he took credit for at Menlo Park, nothing would have been made if he hasn't built the facility and bought all those minds together.

※

Edison helped accelerate the world into a new era. As a man, sometimes his legacy is one of a difficult man who had an absolute drive for his work. As an inventor, he should rightly be remembered as one of the best of all time.

THE STRENGTHS AND WEAKNESSES OF THOMAS EDISON

❧

Edison always had the values of hard work within him and would do so until the day that he died. This can already be seen from an early age after his mother had pulled him out of school, Edison was keen to read and take on all the knowledge he could. While other children would have had their distraction, Edison would have had his nose into a book.

❧

This dedication to hard work led him to be working on the trains at 12 years old and would eventually get him a job for Western Union. Not content with the working life, Edison experimented while on the train and continuously looked for ways to improve the world around him. Once he earned a handsome sum of money, he didn't stop and used the funds instead to build Menlo Park.

From there, he would create a factory of invention and take his work across the country, before building another research facility. He would often work in 60 hour spells only taking a cat nap in between and would often work from the moment he got up till the moment he went to sleep. That hard work helped him to start from nothing to becoming a man still remembered well over 80 years after his death.

His story is also one of overcoming the difficulty. From a very early age, he had developed hearing loss, and many could have seen it as a sign to give into a challenging world where he struggled with one of his senses. Instead, he saw it as a blessing and enjoyed the solitude that it provided. Edison never let his disability hold him back, which is even more incredible considering he was the man who invented a device that was the first ever to record sound.

Edison also shows us the value of teamwork. What he created at Menlo Park was a stunning example of great minds getting together to achieve something special. These days, it seems so commonplace with great breeding grounds of thought at the likes of Facebook, Apple, and Google, but in Edison's day, it was the first of its kind. They were able to create products at an incredible speed and allowed America and the rest of the world to speed ahead into the modern world.

Edison's genius did come at a price though - with his obsession with certain things that he just couldn't let go. Idea's like his magnetic ore separator took far too much of his time, and his rivalry with Tesla and the 'war of the currents' were an example of a time where he didn't know he was beaten. That obsession did also lead to some great inventions though.

Edison loved his work, but whether his family loved it was another matter. He would often spend long periods away from home and the hours that he worked meant not a lot of quality time for the family. His work-life balance tipped almost entirely in favor of work.

It may have been a strength in business, but Edison was a ruthless man in many ways and expected a lot from the people around him. He took credit for all the work completed at his facilities, and his ego was an incredibly big one, he was a prominent character who engineered everything about his life to be all about him. Many people weren't credited with incredible work, but Edison was able to walk away with the praise that he didn't deserve.

HOW CAN WE USE EDISON'S STRENGTHS IN OUR LIVES?

As a rags-to-riches story, there's not a lot better than Edison's. For all his faults, the man shows the value of hard work in every possible way. While people may talk about his being falsely remembered for inventing the light bulb or taking credit for all the invention at Menlo Park, it's easy to forget what the man achieved. He was a great mind, but none of that would have got anywhere if it wasn't for his drive and determination. Imagine - what if Edison decided not to work hard? It would have been a great mind gone unused. It makes you wonder what you are capable of if you had the same dedication.

※

It's not just the dedication though; it was the ability to use that hard work to think big and never settle for one thing. He pushed himself to achieve more and wasn't afraid to take risks. He was sacked from Western Union and went to create his early inventions and wouldn't let his disability hold him back.

❧

While not many could ever dream of the man's ego, he did show what could be achieved with a little confidence. He made bold claims and did everything he could to the back it up. Edison showed that if you can just believe in yourself, then you will be able to achieve things that others would have previously have thought impossible.

❧

He also taught the world the value of teamwork. He worked very well in a group and creating an environment where everyone could feed off each other was a brilliant way to get things done at an amazing pace. Great minds shouldn't always be left alone to think; sometimes they need a soundboard and someone to bounce off. Edison was never afraid to take on someone else's ideas and use them for the sake of invention.

❧ XIII ☙
REMEMBER HIM FOR THE RIGHT REASONS

"I find my greatest pleasure, and so my reward, in the work that precedes what the world calls success."

— THOMAS A. EDISON

❧❀☙

It is always interesting how history remembers specific facts and not others. Many facts can get muddled over a time where people get forgotten or falsely credited. Just like people thinking that Henry Ford invented the first automobile, or that Alexander Graham Bell invented the telephone or that Galileo invented the telescope.

❧❀☙

Thomas Alva Edison seems to be remembered these days as

either the man who invented the light bulb or the man who didn't. Without knowing any more about him, you are either giving him false praise for something he didn't do or not taking into account all the other work that he did.

In truth, Edison was a man who invented a lot of things while bringing about incredible advancements in many other things. With the stock ticker, the telegraph, the light bulb, and motion picture, he may not have invented them, but he improved on them beyond any recognition. They wouldn't be the technologies they were today without Edison's great mind working on them.

What he did invent was astounding too. The phonograph was a truly remarkable breakthrough, and he can claim to be the first person ever to hear recorded sound isn't something that should be underestimated. His other inventions helped change the world around him and bring about a modern age in technology.

Edison is perhaps one of the most misunderstood minds over the last few centuries; it's interesting to see what his reputation has become today. He will forever be known by many as the inventor of the light bulb, but it would be even more impressive to be known as the first person have made a recorded sound, which he actually did.

At Menlo Park, Edison also changed the way that he thinks about teamwork and invention. He showed that bringing great minds together can create great things. You look at Google's '***Googleplex***' facility in California, and you can't help but see it as a modern interpretation of what Edison achieved at Menlo Park.

Edison is rightfully remembered as one of the greatest inventors of all time, but often for the wrong reasons. The next time someone mentions that Edison invented the light bulb, you can put them right and tell them what he did do. And the next time someone mentions that Edison shouldn't be given credit as he didn't invent the light bulb, you can also inform them of all the great things he should be given credit for.

Edison gave the world light, and he gave the world sound. It is an incredible legacy for a man who's rather fled from Canada, was turned away from school for being addled, and had severe hearing difficulties. He achieved incredible things and did it all through hard work. A misunderstood man in many respects, but one of the greatest to have ever lived.

XIV
THE BEST BOOKS ON THOMAS EDISON

- Thomas Edison: Inventing the Modern World – Alexander Kennedy – A highly acclaimed book about how the man changed the world.
- Edison and the Rise of Innovation – Leonard De Graaf – A look at how Edison changed the way that we think about invention and innovation.
- The Wizard of Menlo Park: How Thomas Alva Edison Invented the Modern World – Randall E. Stross – A look at how the world that Edison was born in was so vastly different to the world he died in.

Copyright © 2018 by Kolme Korkeudet Oy

All rights reserved.

No part of this book may be reproduced in any form or by any electronic or mechanical means, including information storage and retrieval systems, without written permission from the author, except for the use of brief quotations in a book review.

YOUR FREE EBOOK!

As a way of saying thank you for reading our book, we're offering you a free copy of the below eBook.

Happy Reading!

GO WWW.THEHISTORYHOUR.COM/CLEO/

Made in United States
North Haven, CT
21 December 2022